Advance Praise for
CAMPUS CALM UNIVERSITY

—— ⓖ ⓖ ⓖ ——

"It's hard to believe that Maria Pascucci is less than a decade out of college. She writes with the wisdom and sympathy of an elder and the wit and coolness of her generation. Speaking with the assurance born of personal experience, Maria extends a most welcome hand to the pressured, stressed-out and frequently impaired students inhabiting our high schools and colleges. She is direct, honest, helpful and encouraging; her blueprint for reclaiming life comes not a moment too soon. I highly recommend her book for every high school and college student and also for parents who need to understand the costs to their children of our high-stakes, high-pressure culture."

> — **Madeline Levine, Ph.D.**, author of *The Price of Privilege: How Parental Pressure and Material Advantage are Creating a Generation of Materialistic and Unhappy Kids*

—— ⓖ ⓖ ⓖ ——

"College is simply one chapter in life's journey, and a grade point average is little more than a sentence in that chapter. Obsessing over this or any single aspect of the higher education process robs students of the fun, richness and true educational benefits available by fully engaging in the overall college experience. Maria Pascucci has created a blueprint that will help students capture the true joy that should permeate every part of going to college. Her advice is invaluable for current and future college students ... and great counsel for all of us who may from time to time lose sight of what is really important in life."

> — **Mark Jacobs**, executive vice president of College Parents of America

—— ⓖ ⓖ ⓖ ——

"Campus Calm is way ahead of its time—an organization that recognizes that today's students are incredibly high achieving and also totally overworked and overwhelmed. Accolades and A's are not what life, ultimately, is about. *Campus Calm University* reminds us to enjoy the view and teaches us how."

> — **Courtney E. Martin**, author of *Perfect Girls, Starving Daughters: The Frightening New Normalcy of Hating Your Body*

——— ◎ ◎ ◎ ———

"Maria Pascucci has created a 'calming force' for young adults who need a deep breath from today's hectic, crazy world. *Campus Calm University* is a true resource for students who need a dose of what's really important—their health and happiness. In today's high pressure, 'must be everything to everybody' world, it's easy to forget to take care of your most important asset—yourself! Kudos to Maria for helping to keep our priorities straight!"

> — **David Mammano**, founder and publisher of *Next Step Magazine*

——— ◎ ◎ ◎ ———

"*Campus Calm University* is an excellent resource for students to put academics, health and life into perspective. With honesty and insight, Maria Pascucci brings much-needed attention to the emotional well-being of high school and college-age students and encourages stress reduction strategies that are highly aligned with research on resiliency, motivation and health. This is a thoroughly enjoyable must-read, not only for students, but also for their parents and teachers who would benefit from the wisdom in these pages."

> — **Roxana Marachi, Ph.D**, Assistant Professor of Educational Psychology, Teacher Education, San José State University, CA

——— ◎ ◎ ◎ ———

"As a professor, I wish every one of my students would read *Campus Calm University* before attending class. Maria's book is guaranteed to give any student a four-year head start on his or her peers, time the average student can't afford to waste. This book is indispensable."

> — Professor **Joe Martin**, author of *Good Teachers Never Quit, Let Your Leadership Speak* and *Tricks of the Grade*

"*Campus Calm University* is the perfect recipe to let go of stress and unhealthy attitudes and relish your college experience for the fun journey of learning that it is. I always tell the students I speak to that their major purpose during the years until graduation is to simply enjoy them, for they will never again have the opportunity for unfettered exploration of who they are and what they want to do. And at last, Maria Pascucci has provided an inspirational, easy-to-follow road map to help them do just that."

> — **Alexandra Levit**, author of *How'd You Score That Gig?– A Guide to the Coolest Careers and How to Get Them*

"As someone who had a physical and mental breakdown during my final semester in college, I wish I'd had *Campus Calm University* to maintain balance in and control of my life. We all have stress, and it affects each of us in different ways, but it's important to manage it with a healthy approach. *Campus Calm University* will help you do just that."

> — **Heather R. Huhman**, founder & president of Come Recommended

"Through Maria Pascucci's writings, one can find the true "secrets" to understanding how perfectionism, low self-esteem and a loss of sleep and nutrition will affect all aspects of a person's life. *Campus Calm University* ultimately speaks that a healthy, happy life filled with love and gratitude is not the key to success, but success itself."

> — **Alex Jordan**, 16, high school junior

"Maria Pascucci deserves a standing ovation for addressing topics like student anxiety, poor self-worth and perfectionism in an engaging, even humorous way that young adults can relate to. *Campus Calm University* is the ultimate resource to help stressed-out students. I encourage every parent to give a copy of this amazing book to their college bound children."

> — **Nancy Barry**, speaker and author of *When Reality Hits: What Employers Want Recent College Graduates to Know*

"*Campus Calm University* should be handed out as every student walks into freshman orientation. Maria's personal story and genuine tone make her one of the most relatable authors out there today. Her message is sure to make all students who read remind themselves they are 'good enough.' If you're a student in college, run—don't walk—to the nearest book store and pick up *Campus Calm University*; it's a must-read."

> — **Stacy Nadeau**, motivational speaker and Dove model, Campaign for Real Beauty

"*Campus Calm University* meets a very real need in college students—finding a balance between performance, pressure, permission to be yourself, power to follow your dreams and wholehearted participation in the college experience. This is a 'must have' for college students, parents and educators!"

> — **Beverly Coggins**, professional organizer, author of *Three Steps to Time Management for the College Student*

"*Campus Calm University* should be mandatory reading for EVERY college student. This book addresses the issues that aren't covered in freshman orientations or any college classes. Maria's honesty will ease the minds of stressed-out students and anyone who is not feeling 'good enough.' I highly recommend it to college students and their parents who want to learn 10 mindsets to create true happiness and fulfillment."

> — **Christine Hassler**, author of *20 Something Manifesto: Quarter-Lifers Speak Out about Who They Are, What They Want and How to Get it*

───── ⓖ ⓖ ⓖ ─────

"*Campus Calm University* is the ultimate resource for those savvy students who want to be in-the-know. It's not only packed full of great advice, but it's such a fun read! Maria literally had me laughing at the turn of every page with her quick wit and wonderfully sarcastic wisdom. It's an absolute must-read for every student!"

> — The Résumé Girl, **Lauren Hasson**, author, speaker, coach and writer

───── ⓖ ⓖ ⓖ ─────

"Maria Pascucci's *Campus Calm University* should be essential reading for all college students today. I wish it had existed when I was in school. With a warm, authentic voice, Maria helps stressed-out college students deal with issues from perfectionism to low self-esteem to fear of failure. This book is bound to help so many young people live happier, healthier lives—and it will help parents and administrators understand and support the college students they care about."

> — **Lindsey Pollak**, author of *Getting from College to Career: 90 Things to Do Before You Join the Real World*

───── ⓖ ⓖ ⓖ ─────

"Five out of five stars. I just finished Maria's book, and it is excellent! Between her years of wisdom and interviews with experts, she shares great advice I wish I had heard when I first started at Stanford University. Every student should read this book so they can balance striving for success with living a healthy lifestyle."

> — **Monte Malhotra**, college student, author of *The Young Investor's Guide to Retiring Young*

"Maria gives you her credible commonsense advice as a result of her own college experiences. With her help, you'll realize that you're not alone and that you can handle your challenges calmly and with grace. You'll also benefit from the wisdom of Maria's Campus Calm experts featured in *Campus Calm University* to begin living a happy and fulfilling life right now. Keep this book handy—you'll refer to it often."

> — **Barbara McRae**, MCC, founder of Teen Frontier International

CAMPUS CALM UNIVERSITY

The College Student's 10-Step Blueprint
to Stop Stressing &
Create a Happy, Purposeful Life

BAKER COLLEGE OF
CLINTON TWP. LIBRARY

By: Maria Pascucci
Founder & President,

Campuscalm.com

Campus Calm University
The College Student's 10-Step Blueprint to Stop Stressing
& Create a Happy, Purposeful Life

Editor: Lori Mortimer
www.lorimortimer.com

Illustrations: Jeremy Stock
jeremymstock@mac.com

Indexing: Christine Frank & Associates
www.christinefrank.com

Design and Layout: Shaun M. Maciejewski, Creative Type Co.
www.creativetypeco.com

Printing and Binding: Lightning Source
www.lightningsource.com

Library of Congress Control Number (LCCN): 2008909148

Second Printing, September 2009

ISBN-13: 978-0-9821167-2-2

" **Happiness cannot be traveled to, owned, earned, worn or consumed. Happiness is the spiritual experience of living every minute with love, grace, and gratitude.** "

– Denis Waitley

Calm Beginnings ...

Hi everyone! My name is Maria Pascucci and I'm the founder and president of Campus Calm and the International Campus Calm University Student Association. I created Campus Calm to help students better manage the type of stress that I graduated with eight years ago. In 2001, I was sitting where all of you are today. I was a Canisius College girl who loved life as a student; I loved my classes, I loved discussing history and politics and social movements and feminism and writing—the list goes on and on. I had huge dreams for my future and I wanted to be a leader in everything I did, and I thought that multiple majors and perfect grades were my ticket to success.

"Could you please close your office door," I whispered to my college career counselor eight years ago. I was a new college graduate with 22 years of self-imposed pressure and expectations bubbling to the surface. Behind closed doors, I spilled my big, fat, ugly secret.

"I'm *not* good enough," I wailed to my counselor, my head hanging in shame. Then the floodgates opened. "I worked so hard for so many years and I can't do it anymore. I'm supposed to be a writer but I can't write, I can't sleep, my stomach hurts, I can't stop crying, I feel depressed. I needed 18 credit hours to graduate on time so I overloaded my schedule to complete a double major and a minor; I worked part-time on campus, worked part-time off campus—all to graduate *summa cum laude* and now that I have, I feel ... empty."

Empty.

I felt my shoulders drop as the word escaped my lips. Depleted. Right when my career was supposed to be beginning, I was ready for retirement.

"I'm going to be a writer someday when I grow up," I used to tell any adult who would listen, my thick brown ponytails bobbing with my bursts of excitement. At age five, I dreamt of my Pulitzer Prize—Lois Lane was my idol. She wore sexy skirts and stilettos and took BIG risks because Superman was always there to catch her when she fell.

But Lois Lane wasn't absolutely terrified to graduate from college and face all the expectations she'd placed on herself to BE SUCCESSFUL. Lois Lane never battled anxiety, writer's block, chronic stomachaches, depression or the insomnia that I was beginning to experience by my senior year. I cried a lot, I went to the counseling center a few times and I was tired a lot. And my stomach was in knots.

I was not a comic book character. There was no superhero waiting to rescue me.

During my last final exam, I reached my breaking point. I was sitting in an exam room for my favorite class, History of American Women. I heard classmates quizzing each other on their notes. Everything went blank. "What if I blow it and don't graduate *summa cum laude?*" I thought. Forget *magna cum laude*, I had a 3.92 GPA and I was going to keep it no matter what. Otherwise, I believed the four years I had made myself sick over would all be for nothing.

Instead of celebrating the fact that I was graduating and was the first woman in my immediate family to have been blessed with a four-year college education, I ran out of the classroom when my professor started handing out exam booklets, bolted for the nearest bathroom, locked myself in a stall and, for the first time in my life, had a full-blown panic attack. Choking tears poured down my face, drenching my shirt, my neck, my hair. My heartbeat pulsated and I began gasping for air. I curled up on the white and blue checkered linoleum floor—and I didn't know if I would have the strength to ever get up. Amazingly, after about 10 minutes, I pulled myself off the bathroom floor and stood to wash my face.

I remember looking in the mirror and seeing a hollow, soulless reflection staring back at me. I said out loud to that young woman in the mirror, "I'm so sorry I did this to you." I walked back to class and finished my exam. Then I drove home, locked myself in my bedroom and stared at the ceiling.

A few weeks later, I walked across the stage at graduation, the harsh fluorescent light casting shadows on my perfectly plastered grin for the whole world to see. The speaker announced, "Maria L. Pascucci— *summa cum laude.*" My family snapped pictures and beamed with pride.

A psychologist once told me that a perfectionist might have to hit a wall in order to make a personal choice to cut herself some slack. I hit mine curled up on the bathroom floor during my last exam, and then again walking across that stage. FINALLY. Plowed right into it with my little perfect existence. I decided that perhaps it was time I get to know the young woman I'd become instead of chastising myself for the woman I wasn't.

I started working through my rigid expectations through journaling and with the help of a counselor. We talked about how I was really failing no one but myself by never trying new things for fear of making mistakes. My counselor suggested that I try yoga to soothe my anxiety. She said that I needed to practice mindfulness. I shrugged my shoulders and said, "Whatever, my mind is working ALL the time." What my counselor meant was that I was spending so much time always thinking, never stopping to look around and appreciate what was right in front of me.

I bought yoga DVDs and was surprised by how different they made me feel in comparison to the cardio dance videos I'd been sweating to for years. Yoga taught me how to center in the present and express gratitude for all the ways my body and my mind serve me, today. There's nothing like sitting cross-legged on a yoga mat, eyes closed, hands stretched to the heavens, chanting, "I am revitalized, I am uplifted and empowered," to change your mindset about life! I mean, what's a padded résumé and portfolio packed with accomplishments worth if I wasn't uplifted and empowered, not to mention happy?

After college, I initially didn't find all the happiness and success that I had hoped would be waiting for me. I'm thrilled to say that I now unlocked the "secret," with the help of counseling, soul-searching and the 10 mindsets I discovered along the way. The 10 mindsets to *authentic* success and happiness that I'm going to share with all of you right now.

Because the story I've just told isn't only about my story. Every day through Campus Calm, I receive e-mails from students just like you, perfect girls and tough guys all around the world who stress and worry about the future and tie their self-worth to their achievements instead of who they authentically are on the inside.

Someone once told me that we get what we focus on. He said to focus 5 percent on the problem and 95 percent on the spiritual solution. This book marks the beginning of the spiritual solution: to spread a dose of "Campus Calm" to stressed-out students worldwide so you don't have to suffer needlessly like I did. My solution is my 10 student mindsets for a lifetime of authentic happiness and success. Let my solution be your collective solution as well.

Chapter One—*Ditch Your Inner Perfectionist*—offers motivation to stop stressing so much over the meaning of individual test scores and the pursuit of the perfect GPA. You will learn how to ignore your inner critic and commit to enjoying your college experience with a focus on learning and relationship building.

Chapter Two—*Love to Learn*—focuses on all the cool things that start happening when you say goodbye to perfectionism and commit to being a lifelong learner. Tips to uncover your inner lifelong learner are included.

Chapter Three—*Be Passionate in a PG Kind of Way*—teaches you how to infuse joy into your life by aligning your time with the kinds of pastimes and activities you really enjoy. From picking a major that excites you to exploring careers and relationship building, your purposeful life starts with some passion—that is, in a PG kind of way. ☺

Chapter Four—*Find the Courage to Explore, Take Risks and Even ... "Fail"*—helps you to understand that it takes bravery to make mistakes, learn from them and keep going. If you're looking for tips to try new things and get out of your comfort zone, this chapter is for you.

Chapter Five—*Be Creative*—teaches you how you can tap your inner Picasso and be marketable to *any* employer no matter what your college major or degree. Psst, it starts with you being gutsy enough to value your unique qualities—after all, conformity is such a bore.

Chapter Six—*Focus Inward*—teaches you how to eliminate confusion by looking inside yourself for answers when the rest of the world is telling you that "you should" be headed down a different path. Self-reflection exercises are included.

Chapter Seven—*Surround Yourself with Positive People*—provides helpful tips and motivation to start building your life and career success teams today. Note: a success team includes the people in your life who want you to be happy and successful on your own terms. These people aren't there to be used only when you need a favor, though. They are to be recognized and valued for the true gifts that they are in your life each and every day.

Chapter Eight—*Think Big!*—will challenge you to stretch your imagination and commit to investing in your unconventional, sometimes wacky dreams. The world is counting on your generation's Big Thinkers to help solve the challenges of today by providing solutions for tomorrow. Don't you want to use your unique skills to be part of it?

Chapter Nine—*Love Yourself*—reveals the most important mindset shared by all happy, stress resistant people and offers motivation as to why you can never be *truly* successful without it.

Chapter Ten—*Have Fun*—If you want to be happy and successful for the rest of your life, have a little more fun! High five for all you procrastinators, right? Not exactly. We'll show you how to have some foolish fun without hurting your academic career.

Campus Calm and this book don't offer a quick fix for student stress. The answer doesn't come in the form of a magic pill (unfortunately). I hate wild claims like, "Cure college student stress in one sitting!!! All you need to do is purchase my book. Shipping and handling not included." So I will *not* offer any ridiculous claims that I can solve all your problems because I simply cannot guarantee that.

Campus Calm University will help you to *calm* college student stress, though. This book will help you make a commitment *today* to slow down. I will motivate you to ask yourself some hard questions about the kind of life you want to lead and to choose whether you want to make your health a priority while you're navigating through your hectic, stressful student years. You will learn how you can achieve academic excellence while paying attention to your own happiness and well-being. This 10-step blueprint teaches you how to find "campus calm" at any university and embrace the new paradigm of success characterized by joy, passion and purpose. What are you waiting for?

Founding Campus Calm has been about my living my bliss and changing my life. I've overcome chronic insomnia, stomachaches, women's health problems, depression and anxiety by intentionally deciding to create a life that supported my healing. Do I still get an occasional sleepless night or stomachache due to stress? Yes, but now I immediately respond to my body's cues and work to put my life back in balance before I spiral. I am grateful for every hardship I've ever had to go through because each one brought me to the place I am today, able to share my experiences with you.

Enjoy and please send me your feedback. I always value students' thoughts and opinions! E-mail maria@campuscalm.com.

Live your bliss, ☺

Maria

——— ⊚ ⊚ ⊚ ———

Campus Calm University Syllabus

WELL, SELF DOUBT, I GUESS I'LL BE SEEIN' YOU. I'VE GOT TO RUN!
FINE! WHO NEEDS YOU ANYWAY?!? YOU NEVER WERE GOOD ENOUGH FOR ME!
JEREMY STOCK '08

" **Nothing important, or meaningful, or beautiful, or interesting, or great, ever came out of imitations. What is really hard, and really amazing, is giving up on being perfect and beginning the work of becoming yourself. "**

– Anna Quindlen

1 | Ditch Your Inner Perfectionist

You know that obnoxiously powerful voice that whispers in your ear, "You're not good enough, you'll never be successful, you'll never figure out what you want out of life, you're stupid, you're ugly, you'll never please your family, you'll never be happy,"? Allow me to introduce you to your inner perfectionist. ☺

Our inner perfectionist is damaging because, if we allow ourselves to listen, she makes us doubt our worth, stunting our childlike inclination to play, explore, take chances and grow as people. The first step in shutting up your inner perfectionist is realizing when he or she is screaming right at you. Every time you have a negative self-thought you have to be in tune with it and immediately say, "Stop!" Then replace that negative thought with something positive. It takes practice but it gets easier the more you do it.*

Let's use the example of grades.

As a driven student, you value good grades and the accolades that come with them. And you should be proud of your accomplishments! However, if striving to be the best is starting to feel like a burden too great to bear, maybe it's time to set some realistic expectations.

The next time you receive a B on a paper and you start thinking, "Oh my God, I'm so stupid, I should just drop this class right now and take something easier," make a conscious decision to replace that thought with something positive like this: "Okay, a B isn't so bad. BREATHE! I tried really hard, and learning is more important than the grade. This experience will help me grow as a person so I'm going to stick out the class and try to enjoy it."

Okay, okay, I know what you're thinking: "But my guidance counselor told me that grades and extracurriculars matter, and so-and-so didn't get into his choice of grad schools because his GPA missed the cutoff by one point." Or how about, "Focusing on learning is nice in theory, but I have an academic scholarship I have to protect." Or, "I need to secure scholarship money for grad school. My parents will go berserk if I bring home a B, and they're signing the checks for college."

I'm not trying to trivialize the practical pressures you face, the pressures that I cracked under not too long ago. We've been raised to

---

* *If you need some extra help replacing negative self-thoughts with positive ones, check out Appendix B: Ditching Your Inner Perfectionist Q&A with Hilary Silver, LCSW, Mental Health Expert, Campus Calm.*

believe that every achievement we earn is simply a stepping-stone to the next level of success. We stress ourselves out to pad our résumés while rarely, if ever, taking a moment to really question whether the end result is worth the insanity.

Consider this letter from a twentysomething *summa cum laude* college graduate:

Dear Maria,

I just read your story about whether it's worth it to chase the summa cum laude *status. The story moved me.*

I too achieved that elusive 4.0, and in the end, I don't know if it was worth it. I gave up so much to be at the top, and it was a lonely place to be. The many nights that I rejected offers to go out and make friends made me a loner. The people who wanted to hang out with me were only there to copy my homework or wanted me to tutor them.

When I tell people I have a 4.0, they're impressed at this seemingly impossible achievement, but I think it's quite over-rated. I did it to prove to my parents that I was worthy of their admiration and love. I did it to prove that women can achieve the highest honors in a male-dominated field (computer science). I also did it to prove to myself about my own self-worth.

Today, I am happier reaching for goals that are motivated by happiness. My type A personality still makes me inclined to be perfect, but I now know better how to strike a balance.

I'm so glad you shared your summa cum laude *experience with the world. You wrote the things that I could not express.*

Thank you for that.

Best regards,
Stephanie

A spotless success portfolio equals a lifetime of happiness and success? Please! That's one of the most perfectly packaged lies we're spoon-fed from the cradle to college graduation and beyond. Striving for perfection equals nothing but headaches, heartache and a never-ending sense of failure and disappointment.

Did you know?

According to a 2005 survey* of high school students in Palo Alto, California, 83 percent of students say that everything they do in high school is crucial for getting into college. Another 74 percent believe it is all right to suffer in order to get into the college of their choice. Forty-nine percent of students say a B is a bad grade.

As a former straight-A student who graduated from college with a near-perfect GPA, I can tell you that a few B's or C's would not have ruined my career. In fact, lowering my super-high expectations would have made me a more well-rounded student. It certainly would have

---

* *"Stress: The High School Epidemic," The Oracle (the student newspaper of Henry M. Gunn High School), December 14, 2005.*

made me a more relaxed student! Grade-obsessed, I didn't pursue outside internships when my college offered them. I didn't make time for a few extracurricular activities that sounded exciting to me. I didn't make meaningful friendships with other classmates and wasn't involved in my school's community. I can count the number of campus social functions that I attended in four years on one hand. Today, when I receive invitations for alumni events, I think, "Why should I bother attending?" I didn't know anyone on campus except my professors and career counselor. In essence, I missed a huge part of the college experience, an experience that I can't get back.

When I graduated, I was so stressed out I almost ditched my childhood dream to be a writer because I had grown to equate writing with nothing but pressure, deadlines and a misguided sense of achievement. I wrote to make the grade. And I lost myself in the process. As a college student, I didn't write one thing for myself, for the simple joy of self-expression. If there wasn't an assignment to be aced, I felt like my words didn't merit ink. Considering that I have been a writer at my core my entire life and that writing is my instrument by which to orchestrate my dreams, in choosing not to write for myself first, I denied myself my greatest outlet for managing stress.

I'm certainly not the only student who was a chronic stressaholic either! According to the American College Health Association's latest Fall 2008 assessment of college students, the biggest life issue that students report affects their studies is stress. Big surprise, huh?

Shelly's story...

Hi Maria, I stumbled upon your Website while surfing the Internet, and I almost cried when I read your biography. It felt like I was reading my own. I am a junior in college majoring in biology and minoring in chemistry. I make myself sick if I receive anything less than an A on tests. I put my entire self-worth and identity into my academic accomplishments trying to prove to everyone that I am talented. I am an obsessive perfectionist when it comes to school.

Sincerely,
Shelly

Christopher's story ...

I just wanted to tell you how much I appreciated your piece "In Pursuit of Perfection" on the Campus Calm Website. [www.campuscalm.com/perfection] During high school and my first year in college, I suffered some of the psychological damages from overstressing about everything, from academics to eating. I have been working to try to regain control over those aspects of my life, and your article helped to put some things into perspective. It is unfortunate that there are so many students who feel such immense pressure to be perfect at everything.

Sincerely,
Chris

Carrie's story...

Maria, I just read your article "Summa Cum Laude
& Valedictorian: Are They Worth It?"
[www.campuscalm.com/summa] and it was as if I wrote
it myself. Your story exactly mirrors what I am currently
doing to myself. Nothing is ever good enough; a 94 percent
is disappointing. I always feel I should have done this, or I
could have done better, etc. I have gotten to the point that I
am now taking medication to help with the anxiety. I don't
know why I do it. I am sitting here afraid to complete this
huge project worth 50 percent of my grade because I am
afraid it won't be "good enough." Right now, I feel com-
pletely 100 percent burned out and fresh out of any creative
ideas. Why? I have a 3.95 GPA and now I am terrified of
"blowing it." AHAHAH. How can I give this up and not let
it rule my life?

Sincerely,
Carrie

Lisa's story...

Maria, I found your article on the pursuit of perfection quite
helpful and something that I can really relate to. During
law school I worked myself to a standstill in an attempt to
graduate summa cum laude. After achieving this, I was
awarded a scholarship to study in the United States. Dur-
ing my second semester in the United States both my mind
and body finally reached the breaking point and I ended up
in a mental health facility for two weeks. I was diagnosed

with bipolar disorder and I had apparently suffered a manic episode.

This was the scariest thing I have ever endured and I was convinced that I was going to die. It's been six months since my diagnosis and I have had no reoccurring episodes. I think my breakdown could be attributed to pushing myself over the edge to achieve perfection in my studies after other aspects of my life were spinning completely out of control. I could not believe it when I was sitting in a room filled with alcoholics, drug addicts and prisoners, but I realized that in many ways I was not that different from any of those people.

So I am writing this to thank you for sharing your experience online so that others can be enlightened and can hopefully escape having to learn things the hard way.

Kind Regards,
Lisa

So Many Students Stress Over Grades and GPA

According to a spring 2009 poll of more than 2,200 college students across 40 colleges and universities, 85 percent of students reported feeling stressed on a daily basis; academic concerns like school work and grades top student list of stressors, over financial woes even in today's economy*.

---

* *mtvU and Associated Press College Stress and Mental Health Poll, Spring 2009.*

⑥ According to the 2008-2009 "State of Our Nation's Youth" report findings that were released by the Horatio Alger Association of Distinguished Americans, 45 percent of high school students said that the pressure to get good grades was a major concern. These numbers have increased by 19 percent since 2001. In fact, combined with the second most common stress, getting into a good college (33 percent), 62 percent of today's high school students say that high school transcripts are a dominant pressure in their lives. 38 percent say "getting good grades" is the biggest source of stress in their lives.

From the time we grab our lunchboxes, wave goodbye to Mommy and Daddy and hop on the kindergarten bus, we're taught that being a straight-A student pays off in gold sticker stars*. Whether a parent, coach, teacher, or any adult tells us or simply implies it, we grow up believing that our performance in life is not an end in itself. Basically, we perform to be judged, and we believe that our numbers are what will determine our future success and happiness, as if these things are prizes that can be won. We chase the gold stars and buy into myths that cause students to overachieve academically. Or worse, we say to ourselves, "If I'm not good enough or smart enough to get straight A's then why should I even bother to try in school?" Dr. Al Siebert, author of *The Resiliency Advantage: Master Change, Thrive Under Pressure, and Bounce Back from Setbacks*, says, "It takes a long time to develop an attitude, and it takes conscious, applied personal effort to undo or change an attitude." The pressure-cooker reality that you've been living with for twelve plus years does not have to be your reality if you make a commitment to change your attitude.

---

* *Term borrowed from Alfie Kohn's book* Punished By Rewards: The Trouble with Gold Stars, Incentive Plans, A's, Praise, and Other Bribes.

Get Past the Myths That Cause Students to Overachieve

1. Getting straight A's in school doesn't guarantee lifelong success and happiness.

2. Your résumé is not your be-all-end-all ticket to success.

3. An Ivy League education or the perfect grad school or law school is not your only ticket to success and happiness.

4. There is not only one path to fulfillment in life.

What are Success and Happiness?

Take out a piece of paper and a pencil. Write down the following questions: What does success mean to me? What does wealth mean to me? Does wealth equal success and why? Is wealth required for happiness? How wealthy is wealthy enough? Does happiness equal success? Does success equal happiness? Does being happy make me wealthy?

Yes, I know they're philosophical questions bordering on existential ("To be or not to be?" ☺), but they're also very practical, honest questions that we need to ask ourselves, especially if we're linking straight A's to our future success, happiness and prosperity. Just the intentional act of writing these questions down marks our journey of self-reflection. Remember, there are no right or wrong answers to these questions. We don't need to have the answers ASAP—the answers will unfold over time when we choose to seek them out for ourselves.

Alexandra Levit, Campus Calm's Twentysomething Career Expert, wrote me to say:

Maria, I was a straight-A student my entire life, and when I got into my dream school, Northwestern University, I was determined to be just as successful there. And while I did find time for fun, my studies were always top of mind.

I'm not a person with a lot of regrets, but the one that I do have involves my decision to graduate early so that I could enter the job market ahead of my classmates. I was hell-bent on skipping up New York City's corporate ladder as soon as possible, and my goal was to be a VP at a major communications firm by the age of 30.

I wish now that I'd used college as an opportunity to explore—academically, socially and personally—instead of as a mere entry point to my professional life, which I have now had for ten years and will have for the foreseeable future. After a few years, that goal of becoming a VP wasn't even particularly relevant, as, with the publication of my first book, They Don't Teach Corporate in College—A Twenty-Something's Guide to the Business World, *I launched a career as a workplace author and speaker.*

In my speeches at universities, I tell students that they have only four years to enjoy school and look out for themselves, whereas they have the rest of their lives to work and look out for others. There's simply no way college students can know at this age what they want to do ten or twenty years from now. The best thing they can do for their career in college is to try as many options as possible and experiment with what interests them. If I'd done more of this, I might have found my passion as an author sooner.

Get Good Grades Minus Burnout

I recently received an e-mail from Karen, a 20-year-old college student from the Philippines. She asked two questions:

1. Is it really possible to graduate *summa cum laude* without losing one-self in the process? (Meaning you won't become insanely exhausted after four years.)

2. What advice would you give to students (myself included) who are dead serious about graduating at the top of the class?

Well, first off, I want to say that I *love* when students connect with me because it gives me the chance to pass on my hard-earned-wisdom. As someone who did graduate *summa cum laude*, I can say that there's absolutely nothing wrong with being highly motivated. If you have a BIG academic or life goal, and if you want to challenge yourself, you should be commended for it!

As far as answering whether it's possible to graduate *summa cum laude* without having a meltdown as I did, I can answer "yes" provided you do the following four things:

1. Soul-search why you want to graduate *summa cum laude*. Is it because you love learning and want to commit to the highest of academic excellence? Is it a personal challenge you want to take on in order to prove to yourself and others that you have what it takes? Have you always been the straight-A student and believe it shapes your identity in the eyes of others or even in your own eyes? Do you want to go to a top graduate school where the cutoff GPA for acceptance is very high? Do you believe that straight A's will ensure future happiness and success?

Take a few minutes to focus on the questions above and attempt to figure out why you want to get good grades. When you're done, keep reading.

_____

_____

_____

Basically, if your motives are internally driven, if graduating *summa cum laude* is a goal YOU really want to achieve for you, then you're probably going to be less stressed than if you're constantly thinking, "Oh my God, I have to graduate *summa cum laude* to please my relatives and prove my worth, and I'm never going to be happy or successful if I don't ace this next test."

2. Make a pact with yourself to never shy away from an interesting class for fear of not getting an A. When I was in college, a professor who taught European history confided to me that one of her students wanted to drop her class right before midterms. Even though this student loved European history, she told the professor that she was struggling and didn't want to ruin her chances of graduating *summa cum laude*. The professor confided that her student was slated to get an A- in her course by mid-term. It's so unfortunate that the student couldn't enjoy her class—a class she loved and in which she was doing well—just because an A- wasn't good enough. If I've learned one thing since graduating, it's that challenging myself to love learning above the almighty grade is a reward all in itself.

3. Make time every day for self-care. That means getting enough sleep every night, eating whole nutritious foods on a daily basis and not skipping meals or replacing meals with junk food because you're too busy or stressed to sit down and eat a real breakfast, lunch or dinner. I also recommend that you make time for a daily dose of exercise, even if that means a twenty-minute walk to the library to do your homework. Exercise releases endorphins and lowers your stress hormones, so it's well worth crazy-busy college students' time to sweat out your worries. Also, monitor your emotions, and if you find yourself getting overly stressed due to harsh expectations, make it a priority to talk to a friend or visit your campus counseling center.

4. Finally, realize that while graduating at the top of your class is an impressive accomplishment, perfect grades are <u>not</u> your ticket to a happy and successful life. YOU are. Your passion for your dreams and persistence to keep going when things get hard ensure your future success. As far as happiness goes, my friend Nancy Barry, Campus Calm's Recent College Graduate Expert, says, "The happiest people don't necessarily have the best of everything. They just make the best of what they have." Choose to uncover your own happiness and you'll be amazed by what you find was there all along.

> "The happiest people don't necessarily have the best of everything. They just make the best of what they have."
> -Nancy Barry

Set Healthy Goals

If you don't know how to begin setting realistic goals, try talking to a trusted friend or family member, or consider making a trip to your campus counseling center or your guidance office. With a trusted professional's help, you can begin to ask yourself questions like:

◉ What does it mean to be a successful student?

◉ What does it mean to be successful in life?

◉ Do happiness and good health factor into the equation?

If happiness and good health are a priority (and they should be), perhaps you, your family and your school can devise a plan that will allow you more balance and peace of mind as you work to develop a strong sense of self.

Go Beyond Your GPA to Measure Self-worth

Brians's story*...

Dear Maria,

I am a struggling perfectionist who is near a breaking point. I am a freshman in high school with a senior in college mental attitude. I try to work myself to the bone so hard, and now, if I do not get the highest grade possible, I feel so depressed and anxious and upset. It's awful. Today, I got a geometry test back. I was studying hard the night before the test and mentally told myself I'd ace it! The highest I could get is a 105 (the teacher gave a 5 pt bonus) and

---

* *Name changed to protect the privacy of the e-mail sender, who is a minor.*

guess what? I got … a 95! I felt awful when I saw the test grade. It may as well have been a 68. I pride myself on my academic achievements and when I don't get a 100, I feel like I've failed.

My parents are great and supportive but they really don't understand where I'm coming from. They think perfectionism is just something I'll get through and can just stop whenever I want. Sometimes, I don't think they understand how debilitating perfectionism is. Whenever I look at a grade, I feel like it's a ranking of me, my essential self, and if I don't live up to my expected grade, then I fail myself. I truly don't know how to define myself without my really good grades. I worry that if I don't get an outstanding GPA then I won't get into a good college, and won't get a good job and so on.

My parents don't push me, but I feel pressured by my class-mates. If I make one slip, go down a single point, people will say that I am losing my edge and start judging me. I get so mad when another person does better on a test that I studied harder for. I keep making resolutions to work harder, stay more organized, review more often, and so on. My current GPA is a 98.6 (rounding to a 99) and I'm fourth in a grade of 550 kids. I don't want to lose that. Finals are around the corner and I feel like I already have not studied enough and am doomed to not achieve my goals. I tell my-self that if I study hard enough, I can accomplish anything, but it costs so many different aspects of my life. I feel like I can't socialize as often (and I'm a friendly person) because I should be doing schoolwork. I talked to my guidance coun-selor (who isn't that great) who said that I just should take it easy. I can't just STOP and be okay. The thought of a 70 makes me shiver. I try to research different ways of acing tests and studying but then I realize that I could still get something wrong. It's not my study habits that need adjusting—it's my perfectionism. I want to be happy every day (or a lot of days) rather than just during vacations or summertime. My weekends are just extensions of my school weeks. Please help me.

Thank you so much,
Brian

I wish that all high-achieving students could learn that your self-image isn't dependent on how much you accomplish in school or in life. You can't measure your self-worth by your GPA any more than you can measure it by the amount of money in your checking account or your title on your business card.

That was a hard lesson for me. I was THE smart one. I didn't know how to define myself if I wasn't getting perfect grades, winning awards or mapping out my future. I remember when I was in high school; my brother and I were coming home on the school bus (yes we didn't have our own cars back then in the 90s, can you believe it?). Anyway, we had just received our report cards and my brother wanted to hide his from Mom and Dad so he wouldn't get grounded for the weekend. He said to all our friends on the bus, "But I can't do that because Maria can't wait to run home and show Mommy her straight A's." All the kids laughed at me and I was so mad at my brother, but he was right! My self-image was completely tied into that report card. Even though my parents knew there was more to me than the grades, I had yet to discover it.

Here's what I can tell you now: If you view your high school and college experience as a way to develop your unique skills and find out what makes YOU happy in life, and not just as a way to build your success portfolio, a grade becomes exactly what it's supposed to be: a measure of your knowledge in a particular subject—not a way to gauge your self-worth.

The Canisius College of Buffalo

By the authority of the Board of Trustees and upon the recommendation
of the Vice-President for Academic Affairs
hereby confers upon

Maria Laurene Pascucci

the degree of

Bachelor of Arts
Summa Cum Laude

in recognition of the fulfillment of the prescribed requirements and has granted
this diploma with all the rights and privileges pertaining thereto.
In Witness Whereof we have hereunto affixed our signatures and
the Seal of the College at Buffalo in the State of New York,
this twentieth day of May, two thousand and one.

Graduating with honors from high school or college is an achievement you should be proud of. But you are cheating yourself if you measure your self-worth solely by your academic achievements or failures. I made myself sick for what? Three microscopic Latin words on my diploma.

CampusCalm.com

Are You Valuing Grades over Learning?

You know you are valuing grades over learning when:

◎ you've shied away from a class that sounded interesting because you were afraid that you wouldn't be able to get an A and your GPA would suffer;

◎ you've said to yourself, "It's easier to give a professor what she wants to hear than it is to debate and stand by my own conclusions if I truly believe they have merit";

◎ you receive a B or a C on a paper and immediately think about how it will affect your GPA instead of looking to see how your paper could have been better developed or what you need to learn in order to strengthen your points in the future;

◎ you did your best in a class that was completely outside your comfort zone. You end up with a B+ at the end of the semester. Instead of feeling proud of your ability to excel in a new subject, you feel like you failed because you didn't get an A;

◎ you find yourself cheating on tests and papers because it's a guaranteed way of making the dean's list.

There Is No Perfect Way to Ditch Your Inner Perfectionist

I'm telling you to say goodbye to your inner overachiever. Stop stressing over straight A's. Maybe take up yoga or start meditating. Discover your inner calm. What do you do? You nod your head, declare, "I'm going to stop being a perfectionist right now." Then you attempt to perfect the process of ditching your inner perfectionist. Let me tell you right now: if you've been an academic perfectionist your entire life you are not going to find your inner "OM" overnight. Getting an A- on a quiz next week is probably still going to tick you off. It's okay to acknowledge your feelings, but keep telling yourself that it's the effort you made that counts. I first committed to ditching my inner perfectionist about six years ago and I'm still learning new tricks every day.

Don't be afraid that if you learn to relax your unrealistic standards you'll turn into an underachiever. I gave up the pursuit of perfection and I'm still a very high achiever. The difference now is that I don't let my achievements define me, and I've learned to enjoy the process of working instead of always thinking about some end product that should result from my Herculean efforts.

Take this book for example. I could have spent my time thinking about how this book would establish me as an expert in my field, about how much money I could make or how many speaking gigs I could land. What would critics think? What would the press think? What would my family think? Instead, I focused on the message I wanted my book to convey. I focused on the joy of writing, one page at a time, one chapter at a time. I had to get this book out from within me. How much money I would make upon its release wasn't a main motivating factor. I made sure that I was enjoying the process of creating this book and that I was taking in each small accomplishment.

—— ⑥ ⑥ ⑥ ——

Q&A with Courtney E. Martin: Ditching Your Inner Perfectionist

Courtney E. Martin is Campus Calm's Body Image Expert and author of Perfect Girls, Starving Daughters.

Maria: Campus Calm believes that one major part of living a happy and successful life is ditching your inner perfectionist. Could you share a personal story of how this statement was proven true in your life? Have you ever tried to be perfect at something and ended up losing yourself in the process?

Courtney: There's no doubt in my mind that perfectionism inhibits authenticity, and therefore, success in the world. It also smothers joy, which is also a high price to pay. In my own life, I have learned this lesson over and over again. For example, as a freelance writer I am constantly pitching stories, enduring rejection, picking myself back up, getting the lucky break every once in awhile, reporting, researching, and writing, revising, revising again, and then finally seeing my story in print. I realized one day that I was totally present and hungry and engaged in every step of that process, except—you guessed it—the final step. I would get a magazine in the mail with my work in it and just toss it to the side. I realized that I wasn't taking in any of my successes. I wasn't taking the time to celebrate. I felt like there was this hole inside of me that I was desperately trying to fill with accomplishments, but it was remaining empty because, ultimately, I wasn't actually taking those accomplishments in. Now I sit down with every article I publish and read it over, as if I am reading it for the first time, and really take a moment to be deeply proud of what I've put out in the world.

M: Let's talk for a moment about academic perfectionism. Were you a high achiever in high school and college?

C: I graduated *summa cum laude* from Barnard College with a double major in political science and sociology. However, I do have to say that I LOVED my fields. I LOVED my professors. I LOVED what I was thinking and writing about, so it rarely felt like work. It was truly a labor of love.

M: Where is the line between being a high achiever academically and an overachiever? Do you think the line becomes crossed the moment we begin sacrificing our health to get perfect grades?

C: Great question. I think the answer lies in joy. We have to learn how to pay attention to our emotional experiences of our academics. When are you engaged and excited, frustrated in that great, growth-producing way? That's high achievement. When are you tired, burnt out, frustrated in that tattered, growth-stunting way? That's overachievement. Health is heightened when you're

> "When are you engaged and excited, frustrated in that great, growth-producing way? That's high achievement. When are you tired, burnt out, frustrated in that tattered, growth-stunting way? That's overachievement."
> -Courtney E. Martin

in the flow state and lowered when you're dragging yourself through the mud.

M: How can students graduate with high honors without losing themselves in the process?

C: Sorry to sound like a broken record here, but I think that a student can graduate with honors and have a deep sense of self and health if they have aligned themselves with their joy. I also think it is important for high school and college students to stop overextending themselves in a million extracurricular activities (I wish I had done fewer of them in college). It's great to have interests outside of school, but pay attention to what you're involved in because you think you "should" be and what you're involved in because you love it. It doesn't always feel good to say no or miss out on something, but ultimately you will be healthier and happier.

M: Campus Calm believes that if students want to find the "right" path in life, they should meander down a few "wrong" paths first because the right path shows itself somewhere along the way. How did you find the courage to make some mistakes and try new things?

C: I'm with Campus Calm on this one. I have been blessed with a really amazing family that serves as my support system—that makes it easy to jump off a cliff and hope that I land softly. I've taken lots of risks in my writing life; some of them have been hard, some of them have been surprisingly triumphant. All of them have taught me something about what kind of person and writer I want to be in the world, but of course, the mistakes actually teach you more. I also think of this skill as being adapt-able. Sometimes your timetable is not the world's time table and you have to be patient and trust that the universe will provide. That's hard for me, but I'm learning more and more that it is key to a happy life.

M: Do students need to find the courage to fail to realize a happy and successful life?

C: Absolutely. Too many of us young'uns take ourselves way too seriously. Life is short. You have to have a sense of humor about yourself, be willing to experiment, figure out what you don't want to do in order to figure out what you do want to do.

M: Can you explain how ditching your inner perfectionist actually helps students become better leaders?

C: Just think about Reese Witherspoon's character in *Election*. No one wants to be led by a perfectionist, because she's un-relat-able, unapproachable, even delusional. People are inspired by authenticity and resilience. We want to see that our leaders are totally human and also powerfully transcendent, that they have the capacity to relate with our daily struggles and also see the big picture. Perfectionists rarely see the big picture and they're certainly not concerned with connecting to others. What's more, perfectionists are often as hard on others as they are on them-selves. Who wants to be led by someone who is constantly cri-tiquing and criticizing them?

M: What advice can you offer to students struggling to give up their pursuit of perfection?

C: Find a "good enough" role model—someone who has given up perfection to pursue other P's like passion and purpose. Fake it till you make it by imitating them in various contexts of your life.

M: Do you think that perfectionism is different for young men than for young women?

C: Absolutely. I think women are more obviously perfectionist—it shows up in their body obsession, their type-A personalities, their preoccupation with good grades. For men, perfectionism tends to be more about rigidity and bravado. It's equally health-compromising but it looks very different.

M: If a student does have a problem, do you think there is a greater support network established for women?

C: Another great question. Yes, in some ways, I think women have an easier path to healing because people are aware that they're on the path. Men are often pressured to appear invincible, like they aren't affected by the messiness of emotions. I think it leads a lot of men to suffer silently.*

---

* *When I created Campus Calm, I hoped that the anonymity of the Internet would help young men feel safe enough to connect with me and begin to find the help that they need through my Website. Stressed-out young men do contact me, and I'm happy to say that the Internet does help bridge barriers. It's much easier for a young man to visit my Website in the comfort of his dorm room than it is for him to walk through his school's counseling center doors. I hope my site is a first step for young people—a source of inspiration to lead students one step at a time to the help they may need.*

M: If young women and young men both commit to ditching their inner perfectionist, what positive changes do you envision happening on a global scale?

C: Wow, the world would change in limitless ways. I think that people would lead more joyful, purpose-driven lives. Men and women would probably get along better, have happier marriages and be better parents. The whole paradigm of leadership would shift—no longer would voters respond to the performance of electoral politics, but insist on authenticity and connection. Our health-care system would be far less depleted with people ill from all the stress and perfectionism in their lives. People would live longer. We'd all take care of and celebrate our natural environment more. Life would be grand.

Ditching Your Inner Perfectionist Do's and Don'ts

Do:

⊚ go easier on yourself;

⊚ celebrate all of your accomplishments—big and small, public and personal;

⊚ assess whether you're a high achiever or an overachiever. To quote Courtney E. Martin again: "When are you engaged and excited, frustrated in that great, growth-producing way? That's high achievement. When are you tired, burnt out, frustrated in that tattered, growth-stunting way? That's overachievement."

Don't:

⊚ beat yourself up over every less-than-perfect grade—professors give multiple tests and quizzes throughout the year to give you a chance to improve, and most importantly, to learn;

⊚ allow your grades to define you. Give yourself time to figure out who you are in life with or without your achievements.

❝ I have never let my schooling interfere with my education. ❞

– Mark Twain

2 | Love To Learn

When you're not so focused on grades, you can begin the important task of learning just for the sake of learning.

Have you always wanted to take a music elective but could never squeeze it into your schedule? Make the time! Learning can and should be fun. Ask the most influential leaders in our world what the keys to success are, and they'll tell you that a lifelong love of learning tops the list.

So many students ask me, "How can I stop worrying about grades and start loving learning?"

Well, a second-grader who's very dear to my heart recently came home from school crying because her teacher told the class that if they all got 100s on their spelling test that they could have a pizza party. The lively little second-grader received a 93 on the test and "ruined" the pizza party for all her classmates. You think that lesson in bribery is going to teach her how to love learning?

Besides the obvious gripe about bribing children with pizza in the face of a nationwide child obesity epidemic (sorry if pizza is the unofficial food group in your dorm room ☺), this teacher taught students a powerful lesson about the value our nation places on overachieving. A 93 on a spelling test isn't good enough because, after all, it's seven points shy of 100. With weighted averages in high school, even a 100 isn't good enough when your friend two rows over can boast a 105. One high school junior whom I recently interviewed said, "The class list comes out each semester and you try so hard to be in the top twenty. If you're not you feel like a failure." Is it any wonder why high school and college students are so stressed out?

Second-graders may not be emotionally mature enough yet to realize when they're being bribed, but we're old enough to realize it. We're also old enough to stand up and say that we won't stand for it.

◎ ◎ ─────────────

If you really want to win in the game of life, close the board game altogether and find your own path paved by joy and purpose.

───────────── ◎ ◎ ◎

High school and college students, if you really want to win in the game of life, close the board game altogether and find your own path paved by joy and purpose.

A few suggestions to help you get started:

Take a class you're interested in just for fun.
I'm a lifelong fan of *General Hospital*. That's my guilty secret—I'm a soap opera junkie—I DVR *General Hospital* and I could probably count on my left hand the number of episodes I've missed in the past 15 years! So in my junior year of college I took a communications course called An Analysis of Daytime Television. My other professors scoffed at the class, but I loved it. Plus, I did learn a few useful things that sharpened my ability to think critically about the world around me.

Read a book from time to time that's not assigned for class.
I used to love reading just for fun—I don't know if I'm dating myself here, but I used to love to read the *Sweet Valley Twins* and *Sweet Valley High* series and *The Baby-sitters Club* books and Mary Higgins Clark mystery novels. In high school, I read *Gone with the Wind* over the summer just for fun—and that book is, like, a thousand pages. However, once I was in college, I stopped all that and just read the piles of books that were assigned to me. Reading stopped being fun.

Talk less and listen more.
This is one I struggle with because I LOVE to talk and could become a conversation monopolizer if I don't watch myself. Everyone has a fascinating story to share, though, if you're wise enough to ask them about it.

Ask "why" all the time and commit to seeking answers.
My aunt used to tell me that I drove her crazy by asking questions I already knew the answers to. I guess I was destined to get into writing and interviewing people for a living. What does your family say about your quirks? ☺

Understand that knowledge equips you with the power to make choices.

Ignorance isn't bliss; the more you seek to know, the deeper understanding you will have of yourself and the world around you. You'll be in a better position to make the hard choices that are right for you when the rest of the world is telling you that you *should* be headed down a different path.

So don't ever think that learning stops outside of the classroom and don't ever think that learning has to be boring—you learn the most when you're having fun!

Employers Value Lifelong Learners Over Perfectionists

Being perfect in college isn't the gateway to success and happiness; learning and creating relationships are. Building networks and being excited about something does translate into jobs. If you don't believe me, listen to the employers who hire college graduates like you.

> Being perfect in college isn't the gateway to success and happiness; learning and creating relationships are.

When I interview people, I usually could care less about their résumé. On a scale from 1 to 10 the résumé is about a 3 and where they went to school is about a 2. I'm looking for what they bring to the table as far as their passion, enthusiasm and their attitude. I can teach people how to sell, but I can't teach them how to have a good attitude about life.
    –David Mammano, Publisher, *The Next Step Magazine*

CampusCalm.com

*I look for dependability and then knowledge to do the job I am
hiring for. And then after hiring, if too much CHRONIC LIFE
DRAMA persists, then I know they won't fit on the team either.
And no, I don't feel that the name of the college and GPA are
important. I even have a master's degree and I say that.* ☺
  – Sheri McConnell, Founder & President, National
    Association of Women Writers, International Association
    of Web Entrepreneurs

In the words of Joe Kirchmyer, senior creative services manager for
The Buffalo News, and one of my favorite former bosses:

*If I'm going to hire a new college graduate rather than
someone with some professional experience, probably the
most important thing I look for is how they spent their time
in college. Did they do an internship or work part-time in a
related field? Did they build a portfolio of their best college
work? Did they join a professional association? In other
words, did they make an effort?*

*The name of the college carries no weight with me. As far
as I'm concerned, save your money and go to a state college.
But as I mentioned above, show me that you've made an
effort.*

*GPA is somewhat important. I'd like a 3.0 or better, but
perfection isn't expected or necessary for hiring.*

*Look at me while we're talking, not over my shoulder.
Nothing kills an interview quicker than the candidate who
stares off into space with that blank look on their face. And
dress nice for the interview. I'm not saying you have to wear*

a $1,000 suit, just something that fits properly and covers your underwear.

I don't know, covering your underwear seems like a tall order!

Do's and Don'ts to Be a Lifelong Learner:

Do:

◎ create your own sense of calm in a world that's telling you every which way you turn that frazzled is "in" and that stress spells success;

◎ be the rock your friends can hold onto so they don't drown in a sea of pressure.

Don't:

◎ think learning stops outside of the classroom;

◎ ever think that learning has to be boring!

———— ◎ ◎ ◎ ————

Lessons from a Lifelong Learner Q&A with Joe Martin

Joe Martin is an award-winning national speaker, author, professor and retention expert. He's authored or co-authored seven books, including the top-selling Good Teachers Never Quit, Let Your Leadership Speak, *and* Tricks of the Grade.

Maria: Campus Calm believes that one major part of living a happy and successful life is committing to being a lifelong learner. Can you talk for a few minutes about how intentionally choosing to be a lifelong learner changed your life in a positive way?

Joe: When I was in college I learned how to be a lifelong learner. It was in one of my classes. The professor brought in a guest, a young man who had graduated from college 2-3 years earlier and who owned his own business. I was impressed, but my classmates and I didn't pay attention because the guest's words weren't going to be on the test.

But when the guest said he hadn't worked a day in his life since he graduated because he loved what he did, I started paying attention. I started thinking about his success and what he was doing. After class, I stuck around and went to talk to him.

I was a junior in college and I congratulated him. I asked him, "How did you become so successful so fast? You're only in your mid 20s." And he said, "I'd love to answer that, but how much time do you have?" I said that I'd skip my next class just to talk to him! He said it would only take five minutes. Then he asked me to take out a sheet of paper and write the numbers 1-4 on it. He then asked me four questions, which I answered on the paper.

Here are his questions:

1. How many books have you read outside of class?

2. Outside of what you pay for your bills, how much money have you saved for yourself?

3. In the past year, how many workshops and seminars have you attended? Not what's required, just the free ones on campus or off campus.

4. In the past year, other than me, how many people have you asked this question to? How many people have you interviewed about their success?

He then told me to add up my answers and tell him the total. It was zero. He said, "You want to know how I became successful? My numbers are better. If you don't improve those numbers in the next few years and you have a degree in your hand, you will be in the same place you are now. But if you improve those numbers in the next few years, you won't be the same person you are now."

I haven't been the same since. I've changed those numbers and that's changed my life. Where were my classmates? Gone to their next class. I learned more in that session than in my whole college career.

M: Why and how can students begin to love learning for the sake of learning and not just as a means to create the ultimate success portfolio?

J: I'll list three reasons:

1. The more you know, the more you grow. I've learned that from taking that man's advice.

2. Those who learn more, earn more.

3. Learn so you can teach and reach others. If you ever want to help someone else, you need to learn more so you can teach them.

M: What do you do to challenge yourself to never stop learning?

J: I keep writing to teach others because I want to teach what I learn. I think I learn just so I can teach. I watch movies and think about what lessons I can teach from that movie. I try not to waste anything. Every moment is a learning experience. When I go through hard times and troubles, I'm looking for ways to use those experiences in a way that can help other people. Also, I'm a list person. I write down everything—anything I think is intelligent and that I want to remember. I list what I can do to be a better Christian, a father and a human being. I'm in constant never-ending improvement.

M: So many people give themselves permission to "close the book" on learning the second they graduate from school, as if learning is something forced upon them and only measurable through a letter grade. What happens when you choose to stop learning in the school of life?

J: Three things:

1. You stop growing in all areas of your life. You get stuck on stupid. If you don't continue to learn, you'll stop growing, and

you're probably going to harm someone in some way.

2. You lose your usefulness. People stop coming to you. They stop valuing you. We're on this planet to be used—in a good way. If we're not used, we're useless.

3. You set a poor example for children. Children are watching us. I tell my son, do exactly what you see me do. Talk the way I talk. Use the language that I use. Treat people the way I do. Respond to screw-ups the way I do. Look at what I look at. Listen to what I listen to. That puts a lot of pressure on me. When you stop learning, you stop becoming an incentive for children and start becoming a deterrent. I don't hide my mistakes from him. If I fail to learn, I'm no longer setting an example.

M: How do you challenge students to have fun learning and teach them that learning doesn't have to be boring?

J: I became a professor at an early age. My goal was "to not suck." Being so young, I wasn't far removed from the classroom so I still knew what it was like to be a student. I tried to show a connected relevance with what they were learning to a desired outcome, or to drive them away from negative consequences. You find out what they want and what they are afraid of. Students want to have fun. Hang with their friends. Make money. I build on those things. They're afraid of being bored, wasting their time.

My son is learning about fractions and percentages. He's really into basketball, so I tied math into basketball. I ask my students what they love and hate about school. What they're passionate about. I ask them how they learn. I make notes on how I can combine what they're interested in with the lessons I'm teaching. When I ask them to write, I ask them to write about something they have a passion for. Half the time they're writing about things I don't know about, so then I'm learning something too.

M: You once wrote, "Focus 5 percent on what to do and 95 percent on enjoying the process." How can students learn to enjoy their time in college? How can they not let the worry and expectations of life after graduation prevent them from expressing gratitude for the learning opportunities of today?

J: I have a few points:

1. Major in what you're passionate about. School is a chore when you're bored.

2. Build strong relationships with your professors. They'll help you out. It's not us against them. You can be on the same team.

3. Get involved on campus and leave a legacy. If you go through college passively, opportunities pass you by. Leave something behind. Find something you feel you can make a difference in. It's not for the résumé. It's for the contribution. If you couldn't put something on your résumé, if you couldn't talk about it, would you still do it? That's the test to see if your heart is in it.

> ◎ ◎ ─────────
> "If you couldn't put something on your résumé, if you couldn't talk about it, would you still do it? That's the test to see if your heart is in it."
>
> -Joe Martin
> ───────── ◎ ◎ ◎

4. Don't just do what feels good *to* you—do what's good *for* you.

Students overdose on painkillers—anything that eats up a lot of time that doesn't create success. They get your mind off the professors, the bills, the assignments and life after graduation. Drinking, video games, partying, sleeping around, drugs, television, gossiping, shopping. These are all painkillers. Don't overdose. I'm not saying college students shouldn't drink and play video games. Just don't overdose. You can play now and pay later, or pay now and play later. So why not get the paying over with so you can play later? Have fun in college, but stay focused on why you're in college.

M: Any final "love learning" tips?

J: Use your college experience in and out of the classroom to prepare you for and reaffirm your passion and purpose in life. If you know what that is before you get there, college doesn't become a waste of time. Your classes become something that are preparing you for your purpose and your passion. If you don't find your purpose in life, you will pay to spend your life watching other people live out theirs. Don't believe me? Turn on the television and flip to *American Idol* or *Dancing with the Stars*. If you have to get in the game of life anyway, be a player, not a fan. The pay's better. ☺

How I Stopped Worrying and Started Loving Learning
By: Alexa Roman, Editorial Intern, Campus Calm

I insisted on being a film major in college. I wrote and read film. I breathed film. I ate and drank film. I attended a film program every summer and started a film festival at my school. There was nothing else I could even think to study.

About one year into college, I changed my major.

All of the sudden, I was an art major. (You may be thinking art doesn't sound that different from film, but stay with me.) My parents were so confused. "But you can't even draw! You got a B in art in elementary school!" My friends were even more bewildered. "Does this mean you're not moving to Los Angeles anymore?" Everyone, it seemed, was shocked by my sudden shift of interest.

Ever since I was 8, I had planned to go to film school. My dad is a filmmaker and I spent much of my childhood on set, captivated by the industry. I knew at that very young age that I wanted to be in on the action. I had my entire life mapped out, from my Academy Award speech to my retirement in Hawaii. I worked extremely hard in high school, starting a film club and making movies whenever I could. My life was going exactly as planned when I applied to film schools. In fact, I was accepted to one of the top film programs in the country at NYU's Tisch School of the Arts.

Because of a scholarship, I ultimately decided to go to Ithaca College, a smaller and less recognized film school in upstate New York. After spending a year at Ithaca, I realized I was sick of film. One day, I found myself in my dorm room with a reel of 16 mm film and a Bolex film camera and all I wanted to do was take a nap.

It was then that I decided to transfer. I wanted to rediscover my passion for film or even just my passion for learning and experimenting. All of the sudden, my great plan was turning into a nightmare, so I jumped ship.

When I left Ithaca, I looked for a school that would really challenge me in more ways than one. I ended up at Emory University in Atlanta, a much more prestigious liberal arts school. Although my career goal was still to become a filmmaker, I realized that I could still follow the same career path without following a prescribed educational path. In fact, it might even enhance my career to do so.

I had switched my major to art because I wanted to expand my interests beyond film. I had always loved art even though I had absolutely no talent for it. I thought that art would make a great compliment to film because they are related but have completely different modes of thinking and working.

So, I went to the chair of the Visual Art Department and informed her of my decision.

Me: "I want to be an art major."

Katherine: "All right. Do you have any experience with art?"

Me: "Not really."

Katherine: "Do you have a portfolio?"

Me: "No, I can't draw."

Katherine: "You can't draw?"

Me: "No, but see, that is the challenge. I was a film major and I learned how to make movies. Now, I want to learn how to draw."

Katherine: "Well, that's not usually how it works. Why don't you take an art class and see how you like it?"

Fade in: First day of Drawing and Painting 1. As I sit in the art studio among strangers, I remember what it was like to be an overachiever in the Film Department. Although I was nervous, I thought about how Emory's visual art program was only one year old. How hard could this be?

Cut to: B- in Drawing and Painting 1.

Just as filmmaking had shaped my early identity, my struggle to be an artist began to define my life. When people asked about my major and I told them, they assumed that I was a great artist. I would then casually say, "No, I'm going to be a filmmaker. I'm just studying art, but I'm bad at it."

Visual Art and Art History, which is the title of my joint degree, turned out to be an uphill battle, but I learned more about myself in those three years at Emory than I ever did in the ten years previous. No one seemed to care that I was not naturally an artist. With each year, I became more confident of my abilities and my knowledge of my major. I found myself in the art studio on the weekends, painting for hours and enjoying the time I spent there. Not only did I enjoy the process, but I could appreciate what I had created. Slowly, others seemed to respond to my work as well.

Although my parents, friends and teachers had been slightly wary of this new plan, they grew to be extremely supportive once they saw my effort and growth. The chair of the department, Katherine Mitchell, whom I had sat with three years earlier, became one of my biggest cheerleaders. Not only did I manage to do well in my major, but my passion led me to write one of the first honors theses in the Visual Arts program.

Now that I have graduated, I look back fondly on my years at Emory. I opened my eyes wider when I began studying art. Taking on a completely new challenge can help you in ways you cannot imagine, even if it seems insurmountable. The more different, the better, even if it's just one class.

After graduation, I moved to Los Angeles to pursue film. However, I decided to alter the path slightly. I merged my interest in art and film by working in the Art Department on the television show *Dexter*, which involves all of the production design. If it weren't for pushing myself outside my comfort zone, I would probably still be inside the neat little box I had made up for myself, taking a nap.

Quiz: Are You a Lifelong Learner?
By: Kristen Szustakowski, Editorial Intern, Campus Calm

What would you do in the following situations? Do your choices reflect a lifelong learner inside you?

1. It's ten o'clock on a Wednesday night. You've been studying all evening for your test tomorrow morning, and if you look at your notes one more time, you're going to scream! You're about to switch gears by getting a head start on homework for another class when your roommate informs you there's a TV special on mummies about to start. You're a sucker for that kind of thing!

What are your plans that night?

_____

_____

2. It's time to sign up for final presentations in your Critical Reading class. Two topics are left to choose from: Marxism, which you know perfectly well. You wouldn't even have to do any research. It's a guaranteed A. Or Formalism, which you don't know much about but thought was pretty interesting in class.

What is your presentation about?

_____

_____

3. You're hanging out with your significant other, trying to decide what to do that afternoon. It's down to snowboarding, which you're awesome at and haven't done in a while, or a game of chess, which you've never played.

What are your plans for the afternoon?

_____

_____

4. You're reading the newspaper one day when you notice ads for two jobs you're interested in. Job #1 is at Subway, where you worked your way up to assistant manager before you had to leave for college. You already know all there is to sandwich making so it wouldn't take long to regain manager status and earn a good paycheck. Job #2 is at the Society for the Prevention of Cruelty to Animals (SPCA). You've never had pets before, not even a fish, but there's something about puppies and kittens that makes you want to endure all those hours of training.

Where are you working?

_____

_____

5. You're going out to eat with a bunch of friends who have brought their own friends you've never met. As everyone is sitting down at the table, you realize you have a choice of where to sit, next to your best friend or next to a total stranger you know nothing about but who seems friendly.

Where are you sitting?

_____

_____

Reviewing Your Choices:

Q1. If you've been studying all evening, you deserve a break! A break doing something you enjoy, not just more homework. By setting down your studies to indulge in something you love, and something that's going to expand your knowledge in a topic of interest, you're tapping into that lifelong learner inside you. So grab some popcorn and turn on that mummy special. You deserve to learn about whatever you want!

Q2. Doing a presentation on an easy topic where you're guaranteed an A might be good if you're stressed for time, but if you can, challenge yourself. Choosing a topic you're not familiar with will broaden your knowledge. Not to mention you'll probably be prouder completing a challenging task than a task you already knew you could ace.

Q3. As much as you're dying to show off your snowboarding skills to your significant other, learning something new has its benefits too. You never know what your passions are until you give them a try. So take a sample of everything life has to offer! You might just fall in love with chess.

Q4. There is always more out there than what you've experienced so far. You might be an expert sandwich artist at Subway, but what else can you do? Probably just about anything you put your mind to. So if there's a job that's catching your eye, go for it. All you need is a lifelong learner inside of you that's willing to give anything a try.

Q5. Look at every person like a teacher. That friend sitting next to you knows something you don't. That friend sitting next to you has experienced something you haven't. By meeting new people, by talking, by listening, you are learning all sorts of lessons and gaining all sorts of knowledge that go far beyond what you'll learn from any school. If you become genuinely interested in the people around you, you will be learning for the rest of your life.

❝ Passion is energy. Feel the power that comes from focusing on what excites you. ❞

– Oprah Winfrey

3 | Be Passionate in a PG Kind of Way

Sorry, I don't mean X-rated Daytime Emmy-worthy passion. When I say, "Be passionate," think of how joyful you feel when you start aligning your time with the kinds of pastimes and activities that you really enjoy.

So how does this apply to high school and college and later in your career?

The following example applies especially to liberal arts majors. Let's say that, like me, you love English and history, but you're afraid you won't be able to turn your passion into a viable career. You're sick and tired of hearing, "So, you're going to be a teacher," when you tell older adults what your college major choices are. Maybe you've read about the top 10 fastest-growing careers and you figure you'll give one of those a try instead. In a recent interview, actor Jesse L. Martin said to me, "There are no safe jobs. Find something you love and do it despite the economy."

Now, that doesn't mean you shouldn't be practical at all. As someone who did choose an unconventional career, I can tell you that when you do what you love, play to your strengths and invest in the right mentors, the money *will* follow. If you want an unconventional career, or any career for that matter, you first have to do a little exploring to see if it's a good fit.

> **When you do what you love, play to your strengths and invest in the right mentors, the money *will* follow.**

How Can You Learn More About Potential Careers?

Answer: Start exploring. Find out about different careers. I always knew I wanted to write but I didn't have a clue how to make money writing. So after I graduated from college, I decided to try out the teaching profession. I put myself on a local substitute teaching list—and discovered my personal hell! If you want a good laugh and some motivation to try out careers, read my article, "3rd Graders Weren't Fooled by This Substitute Teacher." It's on the Campus Calm Website here: **www.campuscalm.com/laughatmaria**.

Another fantastic way to find out about careers is to locate people who are working in those careers and request an information interview. Sounds scary, huh? It's really quite simple.

Here's another example of how easy it is. I used to love reading a weekly column about women in my local newspaper, so I e-mailed the author. I complimented her, told her I was interested in learning more about her career and asked if I could take 15 minutes of her time to ask a few questions.

Well, that truly **awesome** lady gave me an hour and a half of her time, took me to lunch and introduced me around the newsroom. Today, she's one of my biggest champions. And when I applied for a part-time job as an advertising copywriter for *The Buffalo News* in 2003, this lady hand delivered my résumé to my future boss and told him he'd be a fool not to hire me. Do you think that helped me get an interview?! I worked for *The Buffalo News* for a few years before I launched my own business.

Don't be afraid to contact people and ask questions. Working professionals like to impart their knowledge to students and will most likely love the opportunity to give you the scoop about their jobs. Dream big and choose a career path based on your passions. Trust me, your passion will impress your future employer FAR more than any polished résumé, perfect GPA or name-brand college ever could.

Remember, all it takes is **one e-mail** to someone who could potentially become your mentor for life! ☺

The Passion Payoff from an Employer's Perspective:

When interviewing a candidate fresh out of college I look for a few specific distinctions. The first thing I look at is obviously the résumé; if it is a jumbled mess I instantly go to the next. Even if the graduate does not have much experience I expect the résumé to be well organized and specifically

*formatted for the job they are applying for. The specific
school and GPA does not impress me. However extracurriculars such as athletics and student government show me
the individual has the ability to multitask and effectively
manage his or her time.*

*After they pass the résumé eyeball test I look for experience.
In this case I would expect to see internships. Internships
not only set up through the school, but opportunities pursued outside the campus setting. It's an easy way for me to
see how **passionate** the individual is in pursuing his goals.
In the fitness field particularly, it's very easy to volunteer
your time at local gyms and training facilities.*

*Last but not least would be persistence: I encourage all new
grads to go after what they want. Do not wait for someone
to call you. Make the first contact and follow up properly.
All employers have many arenas they deal in on a daily basis; they're looking for someone to rise above the rest. If you
truly want the job, be sure that one person is you.*

Rick Lademann, Founder, Lademann Fitness Group
www.lfgtraining.com

Passion, Meet Patience. Now Shake Hands and Play Nice ...

Once you've found your passion, you want it, like, five minutes ago, right? After all, we are the instant-gratification
generation. If we want information, why leaf through a
dusty encyclopedia when we can google our questions

and find answers within seconds? Sorry to give you a reality check, but just because we're passionate about a career doesn't mean we'll leap to the top in seconds. If you're passionate about golf, does that mean you're going to tee off with Tiger Woods next Tuesday?

I love when you read a review in the paper about some new up-and-coming actor or musician who was an "overnight success." Please. The review fails to mention the countless off-Broadway plays the actor was in for years, or how many dive bars the musician strummed away in before he was an "overnight success." Success takes time and work. Nothing happens overnight. Do you know how many rejection letters I received before I had my first story published in a *Chicken Soup for the Soul* book? (See "From Crop Tops to Suit Tops" in *Chicken Soup for the Shopper's Soul* if you're curious.) My passion kept me going while my patience prevented me from ripping my hair out.

Christine Hassler, Campus Calm's Twentysomething Survivor Expert, says that passion is a journey. She instructs us to dissect the word *passion*. "If you look up the word *passion* in the dictionary, you will find that the first definition is *suffering*," says Christine. "The passion of Christ is where the word comes from. So what all of us need to remember is that sometimes it takes a little suffering before we can really arrive at our passion and that's okay." Sometimes people also find their passion in their family or in volunteer work. Christine teaches that we don't necessarily have to find our passion in our careers, or only in our careers.

Share the Passion

Motivational speaker Nancy Barry, my good friend and mentor, is the queen of PG passion. One conversation with her will pump you up to do whatever your heart desires. That's why I invited Nancy to share her *Be Passionate* story with all of you ... that and because she's also Campus Calm's Recent College Graduate Expert and author of *When Reality Hits: What Employers Want Recent College Graduates to Know* (an awesome book).

The Power of Passion

By: Nancy Barry, Recent College Graduate Expert, Campus Calm

What if you had a job where every day was a great day? Every day you were on fire because you loved your work so much. What if every day was filled with excitement and passion?

Passion is a powerful emotion. Your days fly by. You wake up excited about going to work. You make great decisions. You get more done in less time. Passion is the fire inside you that ignites your heart and soul.

I've been blessed to find my true passion. After 25 wonderful years in the corporate world, I walked away from the best job in the world to pursue my passion of helping young adults be successful in their careers.

What led me on this journey? In 2004, several of my friends had children who were graduating from college. My friends were concerned because their sons and daughters either didn't know what they wanted to do in their careers or weren't happy in the jobs they landed after graduation. My friends would say, "Nancy, our kids don't want career advice from us because we're their parents. Would you *please* meet with them? They love you and you love them, and they'll listen to you!"

This was an opportunity of a lifetime because one of my passions is helping other people. Every time I met with a recent college graduate, it was such a high for me! I listened to their challenges and offered advice, and they walked away with a renewed sense of self-esteem. The results were amazing.

People kept telling me I had a gift. They suggested I start a career coaching business. I would always say, "I could do that, but if I'm going to walk away from the best job in the world, I'd want to have a bigger ripple effect. I would want to help thousands of twentysomethings."

So the passion pursuit began! I couldn't stop thinking about how awesome it would be to take my passion for helping young people, coupled with my love of public speaking, and start my own business. In 2005, I decided it was the perfect time to leave the corporate world.

My close friends thought I was crazy. How could I walk away from a great job, regular paycheck and great benefits? After all, I already had the dream job. I was vice president of community services for *The Dallas Morning News* and WFAA-TV. I worked for a wonderful media company and worked with an amazing team. How I could I give all this up? The reality is there was no way to stop the passion I had in my heart for helping young people. For months, it was all I could think about.

I've been blessed because my business has been booming since day one. I have the opportunity to speak on college campuses across the country and also help my corporate clients get their new recruits off to a great start. Walking away from the best job in the world has been one of the best decisions I've ever made.

My passion led me to write my book, *When Reality Hits: What Employers Want Recent College Graduates to Know*. I realized there was so much more I wanted to share which couldn't be covered in a brief presentation. During my presentations and in my book, I share the secrets to success—mastering "soft skills" in the workplace. I tell young professionals what managers want them to know and don't have time to tell them.

The response to the book has been incredible. Young adults love the book because it's written in a conversational style, and they feel as though I'm right there with them in a coaching session. So many people have told me they can feel my passion as they read the book. Twentysomethings have told me they started reading my book and couldn't put it down. For an author, that's the ultimate compliment.

As you think about your career path, are you pursuing a career you're passionate about? When people ask you what you want to do when you graduate, do you light up when you talk about it?

At this point in your life, you might not have a clue what you want to do and that's okay. It's possible you haven't slowed down long enough to think about your passions. I encourage you to go to a quiet place (with a pad of paper) and focus on what *you* want to do, not what everyone in your life thinks you *should* do. Focus on what will make you happy.

Ask yourself these questions. When you think about your best days, what were you doing? What makes you want to high-five someone? What gets you so excited you want to call your best friend and tell them all about it? What makes your heart smile? What do you love to do?

The ultimate goal would be to find a job you love. If you're lucky, you'll find it on the first try. If your first job right out of college doesn't turn out to be your dream job, filled with passion, give it some time.

If you pursue a career you're passionate about, wonderful things will happen. For example:

1. Every day will be great. Whenever someone asks, "How are you doing?" my response is always, "Great!" My mom once said to me, "Honey, every day can't be a great day." I said, "It can't?!"

   If your life is filled with passion, every day can be great. Every day can be one of your best days. My best days are when I'm speaking to twentysomethings about what it's going to take to be successful in their careers. Or, the days when I receive an amazing love note from someone who read my book telling me it changed his life.

2. You'll be a magnet. People love to be around people who are passionate. If you're passionate about your work, people will *want* to be part of it. Let them see and feel your passion. People will come

"People love to be around people who are passionate. If you're passionate about your work, people will want to be part of it."

-Nancy Barry

out of the woodwork to participate in an atmosphere of excitement, passion and optimism. Your success will be in direct proportion to your passion. Others will believe in you, trust you and want to support you.

3. It won't feel like work. If your days are filled with passion, it won't matter if you occasionally have to work a 12-hour day. Passion gives you the fuel you need to get the job done. At the end of a long day, I'm still smiling because my day was filled with happiness and joy.

Are you chasing the top 10 hottest jobs or are you pursing a career which will ignite your soul? (If you're lucky, you may find your passion in one of the hottest jobs!)

True happiness comes when you have the opportunity to do what you're most passionate about. Take the time to find your passion. We all dream of leaving a legacy. Picture yourself 25 years from now. What will your story be? Will it be a story filled with passion? I hope so, because passion is very powerful.

© 2008-2009 Nancy Barry

Passion Is a Lifelong Adventure for The Résumé Girl

My good friend and business confidant, Lauren Hasson, serves as a wonderful example of how you can use passion to help you explore careers and find the one that makes you happy. By the way: Lauren's not one for long-winded prose so enjoy her peppy tales and concise pearls of wisdom. I promise you it will be worth it.

Alias: The Résumé Girl

Real Name: Lauren Randa Hasson

Age: Young enough to be your older sister ☺

Location: Texas

Alma Mater: Duke University

Major: Electrical Engineering, Computer Science, and Economics

Biggest Business Blunder: My senior year at Duke, I was on a Southwest Airlines flight from San José to Austin, and I just happened to be sitting next to the vice president of mergers and acquisitions at Google! Needless to say, I was starstruck. This was an amazing opportunity for *anyone* looking for a job. So, I pulled myself together enough to introduce myself, and we ended up having a great chat. When we landed, he said to me, "I really enjoyed talking with you and would like to keep in touch—do you have a card?" I was like a deer caught in headlights. I didn't know what to say. Of course I didn't have a card. I was only a senior in college. So, I wrote down my name and number on one of those square airline napkins and never heard from him again. And I don't blame him—I wouldn't have contacted me either.

Best Bad Decision: When I was 16, I decided I would become a patent attorney—with a little guidance from my parents, of course. ☺ So, I set off for Duke with the plan that I would pursue an engineering degree that would strategically prepare me for admission to a top law school. But, when it came time to start preparing for the LSAT, I had an "ah-ha" moment: law school was not for me. So, there I was, an engineering major, who not only did not want to practice engineering, but now didn't want to use it for law school, either. I had absolutely no idea what I was going to do, but I knew what I didn't want to do—engineering and law.

So, without any idea as to what I really wanted to do, I joined the bandwagon and started applying to investment banking positions along with the rest of my classmates. And the only thing that made me stand out from the crowd was that I didn't have even one finance course behind me. But, I did something right, because I not only landed almost every finance interview I applied for, but also received offers from the most prestigious banks. Clearly, I was doing something right. And my friends took notice and asked me to help them with their résumés and interviewing skills. And that was the start to my writing résumés and helping college students and recent graduates land their first job or internship. And if I had actually known what I wanted to do with my career, then my friends might not have recognized that I had this ability to write résumés and prepare for interviews. So, what at first seemed like a bad decision to pursue a career in patent law ultimately turned into the best bad decision I've ever made.

Tip to "Handle" Parents: Keep your parents "in the loop." I know from experience that the more they feel included, the less they will hover.

Best Advice: If I had known how hard the real world was, I would have had more fun when I was in college.

"If I had known how hard the real world was, I would have had more fun when I was in college."

-Lauren Hasson

You may be wondering how Lauren was able to interview well enough to land finance jobs when she didn't take a single finance course in college. The key, she says, was passion. She was passionate about being a lifelong learner (see Chapter 2). She was interested in finance so she taught herself finance "on the fly," as she puts it. Her finance knowledge was self-taught—she wasn't studying it to ace a test; she did it because she was passionate about learning something new. "I gave myself permission to explore my options and my passion for learning is what separated me from other job candidates," says Lauren.

Your PG Passion Meter

You may be thinking, "How can I tell if I'm being passionate?" Well, sometimes the best answers are posed in the form of great questions. So ...

Are you in love or in hookup mode? Yeah, I know, I wasn't supposed to be talking about X-rated passion, but in this case, the analogy was just too tempting. When you're in hookup mode, it's all about the thrill of the hunt, right? Proving that you have what it takes to score, win the guy or girl, never mind if that person is actually right for you. It looks good on paper and feels good on the surface. Love, on the other hand, takes time to build. You have to get to know a person and appreciate his quirks. Once you go beyond the surface, do you feel that you want to stick around for a while? Even if it doesn't look good on paper, do you want to invest in the relationship anyway?

Now think about whatever college major, internship or career path you're currently pursuing or thinking about pursuing. This might sound like a no brainer, but do you actually like it? Are you hunting for labels, dollars or prestige? Does it just look good on paper or does it feel right in your heart? Once you go beyond the surface of any given college major, internship or career, do you feel that you want to stick around for a while and enjoy what you're learning?

Does your face light up when you talk about your intended field of interest? When people ask me about Campus Calm, I get really excited and tell them about everything I'm learning, who I'm connecting with, and how I'm impacting others. Sometimes I can't shut up about it. I know when the other person starts looking at the clock or yawning that it's time for me to change the subject. What about you? If someone asks you about your intended career path, internship or choice of majors, do you get excited or do you want to change the subject as fast as you can and talk about something more interesting? If you're bored with the subject now, how will you feel five years down the road?

PG Passion Recap:

Do:

◎ align what excites you with your choice of college majors and your future career;

◎ talk to strangers—and anyone else you happen to come across. Ask them about their careers and learn more about their lives. Never stop learning!

Don't:

◎ settle for anything less than what makes <u>YOU</u> happy.

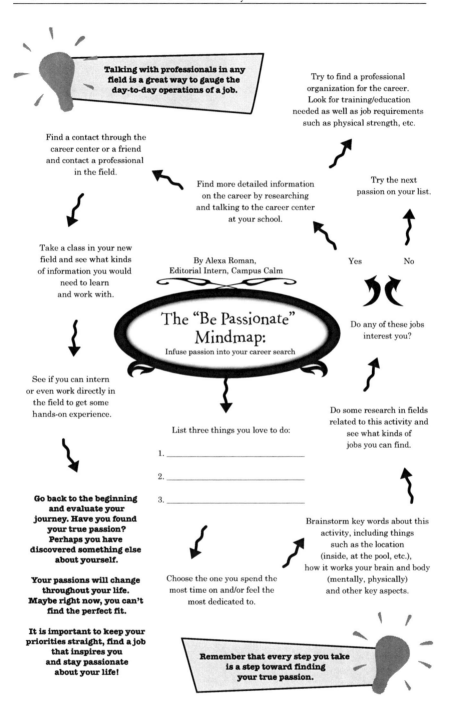

Talking with professionals in any field is a great way to gauge the day-to-day operations of a job.

Try to find a professional organization for the career. Look for training/education needed as well as job requirements such as physical strength, etc.

Find a contact through the career center or a friend and contact a professional in the field.

Find more detailed information on the career by researching and talking to the career center at your school.

Try the next passion on your list.

Take a class in your new field and see what kinds of information you would need to learn and work with.

By Alexa Roman, Editorial Intern, Campus Calm

Yes   No

The "Be Passionate" Mindmap:
Infuse passion into your career search

Do any of these jobs interest you?

See if you can intern or even work directly in the field to get some hands-on experience.

Do some research in fields related to this activity and see what kinds of jobs you can find.

List three things you love to do:

1. _____

2. _____

3. _____

Go back to the beginning and evaluate your journey. Have you found your true passion? Perhaps you have discovered something else about yourself.

Your passions will change throughout your life. Maybe right now, you can't find the perfect fit.

It is important to keep your priorities straight, find a job that inspires you and stay passionate about your life!

Brainstorm key words about this activity, including things such as the location (inside, at the pool, etc.), how it works your brain and body (mentally, physically) and other key aspects.

Choose the one you spend the most time on and/or feel the most dedicated to.

Remember that every step you take is a step toward finding your true passion.

If you want to download and print a larger copy of "The 'Be Passionate' Mindmap", visit: **www.campuscalm.com/book/exercises**

" **Experience is simply the name we give our mistakes.** "

– Oscar Wilde

4 | Find the Courage to Explore, Take Risks and Even ... "Fail"

By "find the courage to fail," I don't mean start failing all your classes and then brag about how courageous you are while you're on academic probation. In our culture, we see messages every day that tell us if we're not number one, then we've failed. Sometimes we become afraid to try something new because if we're not awesome at it right from the start, then we think we're failing.

When I was in high school, I took a photography class and I'm *not* a hands-on person. I took that class because my boyfriend was enrolled and I was a love-sick teenager (btw: he's now my husband so I guess that class paid off). Anyway, I struggled with that class and I wanted

Want to know the right path to take in life? Meander down a few "wrong" paths first. That right path is waiting for you somewhere along the way.

to quit. In college, I received a B on my first paper for a Shakespeare class and again, I wanted to quit. But each time I stuck it out, and I'm a better person for it. Why? It's not like I develop pictures in a dark room in my spare time or recite Shakespeare on the weekends. But knowing that I have what it takes to step outside my comfort zone and succeed imperfectly has made me a more confident risk-taker.

Want to know the right path to take in life? Meander down a few "wrong" paths first. That right path is waiting for you somewhere along the way. As an entrepreneur, I've learned that there is no room for perfection and I have to make many mistakes to reach innovation. In fact, the only way we can ever achieve success in life is through what Japanese engineer and industrialist Soichiro Honda called "repeated failure and introspection."

In order to find the courage to take risks, we have to be prepared in some way for what it feels like to stick our necks out and possibly not succeed on the first or second try. In other words, we need to learn how to develop what my former writing teacher called chutzpah (pronounced *chutzpa* or *hutzpah*), or gutsy audacity. You may have heard the term thick skin. You can't be really gutsy without a thick skin.

You may be thinking, "How do I go about developing a thick skin?" Sounds like this could be a commercial for a new beauty product: "Chutzpah! Get thicker skin in six weeks, guaranteed." I'm picturing some exotic over-makeuped lady draped in leopard print, or is it alligators that have thick skin? Kidding! The only way you can develop thick skin is through the practice of taking risks and making mistakes, one small risk at a time, one day at a time. Here are some suggestions to help get your mind comfortable with taking risks.

Do:

◎ understand that it takes courage to make a mistake, learn from it and keep going;

◎ realize that for every time you're successful in life you had to explore and "fail" somewhere along the line to get there;

◎ develop a sense of identity that's separate from your achievements and your failures. If your whole self-worth isn't dependent on your performance in life, it will be far less scary to try new things.

Don't:

◎ settle into your comfort zone. When you're too comfortable in your routine, it usually means you're not taking any chances. That doesn't mean push yourself to the breaking point though because you're never going to reach innovation when you're being hard on yourself. I just mean take some chances on things that could bring you joy;

◎ back away from a challenge to take an easier but less personally rewarding path—in school or in life.

Afraid of the "F" Word?

Failure of any kind is hard for stressed-out perfectionist students to handle. The very idea of failure causes enormous stress. But the life lessons and experience gained by finding the courage to work through challenges will determine our success and happiness, now and in the future. Consider this example:

As a recent college graduate in 2002, I accepted an unpaid editorial internship with an online teen magazine. I submitted a few of my articles and waited for the glowing reviews that would surely follow. After all, I knew I was a great writer—in fact, I never had one professor tell me otherwise. Imagine my surprise when my new editor, a graduate journalism student at Columbia University, ripped my articles to shreds. She wrote on the top of one, "When Maria *isn't* constantly overwriting, she has a clear voice that's engaging to the reader." I remember thinking, "Overwriting? That snobby Ivy League grad student! What does she know about good writing?"

This knock on my writing style was a huge blow to my ego and an even bigger blow to my self-confidence. I pulled out every paper I had ever written in college (yes I'm a dork, I saved them all in a folder). I read my professors' comments: "Just a model paper, Maria, A+"; "Perfectly executed"; "A pleasure to read." Had my professors been lying to me? Was I really a failure as a writer? Maybe I couldn't hack it in the real world of writing.

I could have quit the internship and forgotten all about that graduate student's comments. I wasn't getting paid for the internship and I wasn't getting college credit, so what did I care? As a perfectionist, everything inside of me was screaming, "Back away now." But this time, I chose to step out of my comfort zone. Looking back, I think the stubborn side of me came out. I was going to show this hotshot editor that I had what it took to be a professional writer. I reread all my editor's comments and tried to look at them as professionally as possible. They were not an attack on my self-worth. They were simply critiquing my writing style.

And a great critique it was. I realize now that I *was* overwriting. I had spent so much time in college looking for the perfect words to prove to my professors that I was talented. In the real world of writing, readers are looking for a connection with a genuine flawed person, a true voice. They want real, honest words, not pompous prose.

When I wrote my next article, I became very conscious of writing with the reader in mind. I kept asking myself if I was choosing words to impress the reader or to connect with her. I cut back on words that required a dictionary. I stopped overusing adjectives and instead strengthened my verbs, the action of the story where real living occurs. My hard work paid off—that hotshot Columbia University editor loved my next submission! She said that I made a real connection with the reader and she was impressed with the way that I had handled the criticism. I was humbled. For the first time in my professional and academic careers, I really felt like my initial "failure" was worth it from the lessons I had learned. The real-life experience paid dividends down the road, even though I didn't earn a salary at the time.

If you want to learn how you, too, can help yourself through a failure and develop thick skin, consider the following advice.

We learn more from our mistakes than from our successes. So the next time you find yourself in a challenging situation, ask yourself, "How can I use this experience to learn more about myself?" Write down five things that you can learn from your challenge.

For example, here are five things I learned through my writing challenge:

◉ I had used what other people thought about my writing to measure my self-worth.

◉ Traditional creative pursuits, such as writing, are subjective and not everyone will love everything you create. That is totally okay.

◉ I needed to learn how to take constructive criticism better if I wanted to be a professional writer.

◉ I was focusing more on trying to impress readers with perfect words, instead of attempting to make an honest connection in a meaningful way.

◉ Sometimes the process of writing is more enjoyable than the end product. I am learning every day that when I actually enjoy the journey of writing, rather than obsess over the end product, it ends up better received by the reader anyway.

Get stubborn. Tell your inner critic that you're going to work through your failure and prove to yourself that you have what it takes to persevere.

Ask questions. Know someone who is able to laugh off mistakes in a healthy way? Ask them for some sage advice on how you can go about surviving failure.

Celebrate imperfection. When you successfully "fail" for the first time, celebrate this Hallmark event. There should actually be cards on the market for this type of occasion. "Congratulations on the successful completion of your first failure. I'm proud of your ability to be resilient and take chances. Good job! Love, Grandma" ☺ (or insert the loved one of your choice). Hmm, maybe I should launch this greeting card line!

Being passionate about our chosen careers, taking risks and learning from our failures allows us to enjoy what Barbara McRae, Campus Calm's Teen Parenting Expert, calls our "Road Trip Through Life."

Road Trip Through Life
By: Barbara McRae, MCC, Teen Parenting Expert, Campus Calm

One thing I knew for sure. I'd attend a reputable college with fantastic opportunities to study and work abroad. This important criterion helped me sort through the college application maze. My high school guidance counselor suggested I check out Beloit College, known for their excellence in international studies. I loved the campus and I was also attracted to their unique "field term" graduation requirement. A "field term," now often referred to as an internship or co-op program, is paid real-world work experience in a field related to your career aspirations that also offers course credit.

What a great way to double-check my potential career path! It's a lot like test-driving a car before you purchase it—just to make sure it suits you. It didn't take me long to decide which school's offer to accept.

I locked on to my target at Beloit College and readied myself to walk down that straight road toward my shining future. I had lived in Munich, Germany, briefly with my parents and now I took to daydreaming about returning on my own. I lived as if I knew I would succeed, because in my mind, it was a done deal.

As a freshman, I enrolled in French, Italian, Spanish and German language classes. It didn't take me long to declare a double major: international relations and German literature. In my sophomore year, I applied for my opportunity to study overseas, the German Seminar, at the University of Hamburg. I had taken the necessary steps to turn my fantasy into fact when I suddenly got thrown off course. The notice I held in my hand turned out to be a rejection letter. I wasn't going? There must be some mistake!

> "Our greatest glory is not in never falling, but in rising every time we fall."
> -Confucius

Perhaps, I was naïve, but it had never occurred to me that I might not attain my goal. I was devastated, but determined to keep reaching for my dream. I remembered what Confucius said about being resilient: "Our greatest glory is not in never falling, but in rising every time we fall." So I made an appointment with the seminar leader, a religious studies professor, to claim my spot. In the meantime, my language professors were as shocked as I was and offered to put in a good word for me.

Evidently, there had been many more applicants than available space. Students needed to be housed by German host families. The decision-makers concluded that since my language abilities were better than those of the other seminar applicants, it wasn't vital for me to participate in this foreign study experience. I was being penalized for having stronger skills than the others? Incredible!

I still don't quite understand it today, but somehow my confidence during that pivotal meeting was unstoppable. Fueled by my passion, I emphasized my language abilities and turned my apparent "weakness" into a greater strength. I outlined how my skills could benefit the other seminar participants, not just myself. All that was left to do now was to focus on my ideal outcome and let go of the rest. There wasn't anything else to do. Several weeks passed before I got the news; then finally, I was "in."

I scored that point, but I wasn't home free yet. I still had to arrange my overseas work program in Munich, located in southern Germany. The college field term office had contacts in several German cities, but none in Munich. Okay, now what? I didn't want to settle for another city. I knew what I wanted, but I didn't yet know how I'd do it.

Soon afterwards, a synchronistic meeting took place with my friend Mark, a fellow international relations major. He excitedly announced that his internship program in Beirut (of all places!) had just been approved by our field term office. In hearing about how Mark had designed his own work/study program, it hit me. That's the answer! I wasn't dependent on my local field term office; I could contact companies directly.

The concept that I could design my own work program overseas was empowering, and I immediately set the wheels in motion. My mother contacted a bank president friend of hers in Munich on my behalf. He suggested I inquire at Siemens AG, headquartered in Munich, and offered to give me a letter of introduction. I believed that with the backing of this senior level executive, I would get my foot in the door at a prestigious international corporation.

After having successfully completed my semester of studying at the University of Hamburg, I took the train to Munich to meet the bank president and collect my precious letter of introduction. I didn't have a job offer yet, but I wasn't worried. My aunt invited me to stay in her home, but I was looking forward to renting a place close to my potential employer with some other young women—one from Austria and the other from Switzerland—closer to my own age. It was amazing how much I learned about different cultures and about myself!

The interview at Siemens went well. There was an opening in their English/German translation department that fit the bill. They offered me the job, provided I could secure a work permit. I didn't think this would pose a problem and said so. But once at the local government office, I was informed that without written proof of having secured a job, I wouldn't be eligible for a work permit. It was a classic catch-22 situation: no job without a permit, no permit without a job.

So, back to Siemens I went. My prospective boss was reluctant to give me a written offer letter. But, I pressed on since I had the impression that he really wanted someone as soon as possible and I was immediately available. It worked!

I was grateful for this work experience on so many levels. Nothing beats real-life experiences. It felt great to have successfully handled unpredictable problems. I loved having a "real job" in a foreign country to be able to demonstrate my adaptability and flexibility in unfamiliar surroundings and unaccustomed situations. I didn't know it then, but my international experience provided rare cross-cultural resources, giving me an edge in working with multinationals down the road.

More importantly, I discovered that while I liked working in a business setting, I intensely disliked translating scientific texts. But a new career track emerged in its place: leadership, specifically managing and developing people. After graduation, I would credit my field term experience for landing a desirable job in Chicago as an employment manager, thereby successfully launching my career in human resource management. Eventually, this led to my becoming what Warren Bennis, nationally known leadership author, referred to as: "A new kind of leader... who is a facilitator, not an autocrat... These leaders realize that they're basically coaches."

Looking back, it's clear that the best-laid plans can fail, if only temporarily. It's also true that a series of unexpected detours can ignite determination and cultivate persistence. My straight road turned into a long and winding road, but I did it! And it was even more wonderful than I could have imagined.

© 2008-2009 Barbara McRae

Barbara's story shows us how we can chart the course of our own lives and meet challenges head on when we focus on what excites us. Barbara was passionate about studying languages and wanting that experience overseas. Her passion for it led her to lobby her case and convince the school that she should be able to go.

Barbara's story also shows us that taking risks and experiencing careers is the only way we will find out what we truly like and dislike. It was through many career experiences that Barbara found her niche as a leadership coach. Is there a college major that specifically teaches us how to be a leadership coach? None that I know of, but that's okay. Focus on the college major that excites you today, because you never know where it will take you tomorrow.

Quiz: Do You Fail with Success?
By: Kristen Szustakowski, Editorial Intern, Campus Calm

What would you do in the following situations? Do your choices reflect someone who is afraid to take a few risks, or are you learning from your mistakes and turning your failures into successes?

1. You decide to try out for the college swim team. After that first day of practice you can hardly move, you can hardly breathe, you have chlorine in your eyes, your goggles broke somewhere in lane five, and to top it all off, you heard the captain comment on how slow you are compared to everyone else. Are you going to show up for practice the next day?

It would be easy to never show your face there again, especially since it's going to take a week of Clean & Clear to restore the moisture in your forehead. But then you haven't given the swim team a real shot, have you? So what if the captain says you're slower compared to the rest of the team? The only person you should compare yourself to is you, and how can you do that if you haven't stuck around long enough to see your own improvements? Maybe you should stick it out another week. You might learn to love the backstroke. Heck, you might even learn to love how green the chlorine has made your blonde hair.

2. It's time to get those core curricular classes out of the way, and you absolutely must take a science. Yes, a science. Your mind wanders to "The Nitrogen Incident" in high school, and suddenly it feels like you're the one under a slide. It's down to Earth Science, which you "rocked" at (I couldn't resist), or Chemistry, which, thanks to "The Nitrogen Incident," your entire graduating class knows you're, well, not very good at. Are you finding fossils or mixing unknown liquids?

You may have made a few iffy chemistry mistakes back in high school, but you're in college now. You're smarter. Even if you failed at something once, build up that courage and try it again. You might surprise yourself. Or at very least, you'll give the Class of 2010 something to talk about!

3. Grandma's over for dinner. You're making her homemade chicken soup. But every move you make is apparently wrong because she's standing behind you with moo-moo and ladle, breathing down your back and cursing out your carrots. When she dips a spoon in for a taste, she coldly remarks that the slippers she bought in '97 taste better. You taste the soup, and even though you've never, ever tasted Grandma's slippers, you imagine they truly would taste better than this boiling mush. You can leave the kitchen quietly, vowing to never cook for the rest of your life, or you can ask Grandma how to make chicken soup.

It would certainly be easier to leave the kitchen and cry, but if we don't learn from our mistakes, we're not bettering ourselves. I'm not saying the ability to make chicken soup makes you a better person, but the ability to take criticism does. So suck it up and endure a few bops on the head with Grandma's ladle. The ingredient you were missing is parsley. ☺

4. You just got your midterm back. There's a C in the top right corner. Oh, how you would love to stuff it in the back of your binder and never look at it again. To burn it behind the residence halls after dark. To flush it down a public restroom toilet. "Just get that C out of my face and let me move on with my life." Except ... you studied, and you don't understand why you got a C, and you do still have to take a final with material on this midterm. Are you going to sentence it to the washing machine tonight, or are you going to figure out where you went wrong?

Sometimes it's painful to examine mistakes. Just looking at that C was probably painful but now you have to dissect it? If you want to succeed at failing, you do. If you sentence that paper to whatever death your mind came up with, you're nowhere further than where you began. But if you stop to analyze what you did to get that C— maybe talk to the professor about the way in which you study—you will not only learn how to do better on the final, you will learn how to benefit from failure.

5. You're working out at the gym when your mind starts to wander to a fight you had with your best friend. You guys haven't spoken in a while. When you think about the fight, you find that you were right in a lot of ways, but you were wrong in a lot of ways, too. In fact, now you wish you would have handled things differently, because things didn't turn out the way you thought they would. You can say, "Oh well. Now, where's that new Kanye West track?" and continue with your workout, or you can really start to analyze. Where's your mind at?

Okay, maybe you don't have to think that deeply at the gym at that very moment, but if you want your failures to be successes, you have to deal with it sometime. It's not easy, but relationships are something everyone deals with every day, and they are very important to us. The mistakes we make in our relationships might be the most important mistakes to look at and learn from, because these mistakes can affect more than just us. If we learn from the mistakes we've made in our relationships, we are making every relationship we have and will have, stronger. Our moms, dads, sisters, brothers, boyfriends and girlfriends, our friends … these people mean the world to us. If we can make the relationships with these people stronger by analyzing past mistakes, we're creating a brighter, stronger, happier world for ourselves, and for all of us.

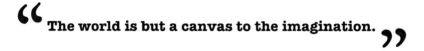

" The world is but a canvas to the imagination. "

– Henry David Thoreau

5 | Be Creative

Every student is unique and therefore brings something completely new to the table. *If* you're brave enough to be yourself in a world
that too often seems to value conformity, that is. Successful students
thrive on creativity. They trust themselves enough to follow their intuition and open themselves up to new ideas and possibilities.

Ask good teachers what they need to see more of in the classroom,
and they'll say students who aren't afraid to be creative. Good teachers don't want you to regurgitate their words back to them on exams.
Speak up in class, spur some interesting discussions, challenge a
teacher's opinion in a respectable manner and be prepared to back up
your argument with your own creative ideas. That lesson in boldness
will carry you to success beyond your wildest dreams.

Even if your creativity isn't appreciated by every teacher you encounter in life, so what? Unfortunately, some teachers do want you to regurgitate their words back to them on tests and papers, but most teachers aren't like that. My advice is controversial, but (*sigh*) here goes: be brave enough to take the occasional less-than-perfect grade and keep your creativity, not to mention your principles, in tact.

Campus Calm believes that creativity is the key behind any successful endeavor, whether it be perfecting your painter's stroke, giving a winning sales pitch or developing the latest computer software program. The word *creativity* is limiting when it is seen only as synonymous with "creative" careers such as writing, acting, dancing or painting. Any path to success requires creativity. More importantly, any person can be creative. All you have to do is believe it and believe in yourself.

Ralph Waldo Emerson, one of my favorite authors when I'm in the mood to really philosophize about life, says, *Do not follow where the path may lead. Go, instead, where there is no path and leave a trail.* Now that's creativity, and it has nothing to do with a career in the arts. Do you see the difference?

How Can You Learn to Embrace Creativity in Your Own Life?

Well, before you can embrace the concept of creativity you first have to define what it means to you. I advise that students ask themselves, "What does the word *creativity* mean to me? Do I think our society values creative thinkers?" Ask your friends, family and acquaintances what they find creative. Make a list of all their answers. Then try to carve out your own definition.

My friend Carleton Kendrick weighed in on the subject of creativity and the creative process. Kendrick is a family therapist, parenting expert and co-author of *Take Your Nose Ring Out, Honey, We're Going to Grandma's.*

Here's what Kendrick had to say:
Creativity is all too often confused with something that someone makes or does that elicits all but unanimous approval. Anything that your mind is conceiving, your mind is creating. A friend of mine who is a poet and former teacher says that he feels really creative when he creates a good test. When you conceive of something, your brain is operating in a rhythm where everything is firing—some people call it flow. It's almost a non-thinking place—your mind is like a popcorn popper. It is not trying to imitate, duplicate or perform for approval.

For example, if you search the word *creativity* at **www.Dictionary.com**, this is one of the definitions that comes up: *the ability to transcend traditional ideas, rules, patterns, relationships, or the like, and to create meaningful new ideas, forms, methods or interpretations.* We can all create meaningful new ideas without picking up a paintbrush or learning how to do the waltz (unless we want to paint or dance, that is). All we need is a good recipe for creative thinking.

Maria's Recipe for Creative Thinking ...

Challenge:

When I was in college, I developed chronic stomach pain that took years to get under control. Part of the problem was undiagnosed food allergies. I discovered through many painful meals that I couldn't tolerate gluten or dairy. So, what the heck is gluten, you ask? Basically gluten is a type of protein that is commonly found in rye, wheat, barley and oats. As you might imagine, gluten is used in just about every traditional type of bread, condiment and baked good on the market. So I had to stop eating many, many familiar foods. On top of that, I had to stop eating dairy?! No ice cream, butter or cheese? If that wasn't stressful enough, I then discovered that tomatoes bother my stomach too, and I'm a sauce-loving, ketchup-carrying Italian.

Did I sit at home and cry about all that I can't eat? Did I feel like a victim? Or did I free myself to address the problem in a creative manner? I chose to think outside of the pasta box (pardon the pun), mainly because I love food. ☺

The first thing I did was assess the problem. For me, any creative problem solving starts with asking good questions. I jotted down the main ones:

◉ What are my preconceived notions about food—how it should look and taste?

◉ How will my attitudes about food and cooking adapt?

◉ What can I eat and what must I avoid?

◉ How will I learn to cook in a new way?

⊚ What will my family and friends think?

⊚ How will I interact at social gatherings?

⊚ How will I respond to ignorant people who assume I'm on a fad diet?

⊚ How will I afford to purchase specialty foods?

Once I had the questions, I needed to learn how I could find answers.

The creative thinker's recipe ...

There are *no* recipes.
If you want to spur creative thought processes, the first thing you have to do is throw out the rule book. People have preconceived notions about how a problem should be tackled. Conventionally, you go to the recipe book and follow the instructions that are already laid out for you. Well, how are you ever going to arrive at anything unique that way?

Start wherever you are. Take any first step that you're able to make in your current situation. If you can't move forward, take a step to the side. I never liked to cook, so the idea of cooking specialty foods sounded terrifying. But instead of dwelling on all the negatives, I gave myself permission to close my traditional cookbooks and start from scratch, testing one new food at a time. I gave myself permission to experiment with foods and flavors until I came up with safe meals I liked. **Bonus:** Experimenting with cooking saves money because I don't have to buy overpriced prepared specialty foods at the grocery store. **Point:** When we allow ourselves to challenge the rules, we give our minds the permission it needs to start thinking laterally, which is how the creative process begins.

Flexibility is key.

Not yoga pretzel flexibility, of course, but mental flexibility. In order to be creative we must challenge ourselves to see the world as full of possibilities and not limitations. We can't think of our options as being either/or. There is no way I could have been creative when dealing with my food allergies if I had said to myself, "Either I give up all my favorite foods or suffer the stomach pain." Instead of these no-win options, I chose door C, which was to learn how to experiment with different foods and develop new favorites.

> In order to be creative we must challenge ourselves to see the world as full of possibilities and not limitations.

I discovered that I like almond milk more than I like cow's milk. I discovered that I like peanut butter Thai pasta almost as much as I like traditional pasta sauce, and I discovered that rice pasta noodles taste about the same as regular white pasta. I also discovered that my intestines healed and my sinuses cleared up when I changed my diet and that my new way of cooking was much healthier. When I cook, I don't look at my food allergies as limitations—they're challenges that afford me the opportunity to be creative with my cooking.

My baby cousins love to play pretend restaurant. I sit down and they use their Fisher-Price cook set to prepare me any meal that I want. Since it's pretend, I ask for all my favorite foods that I can no longer eat, like pizza and hot fudge sundaes. I don't tell them, "You have to do this" or "You can't do that." I just let them pretend and see how outrageous their play can become. We all need to pretend more. **Point:** Whenever you're stuck with either/or thinking, close your eyes and pretend there are more possibilities. What do you see?

No recipes = an opportunity for mishap.

Remember Chapter 4—Find the Courage to Explore, Take Risks and Even ... Fail? Well, if you want to harness your creativity, you have to be willing to accept the occasional mishap. **Point:** You have to give yourself permission to come up with lame ideas to arrive at the not-so-lame. Or in my case, I have to be willing to accept the occasional soggy gluten-free, dairy-free pancake so I can whip up an edible breakfast.

When life hands you inedible pancakes, make muffins.

I once prepared gluten-free buckwheat pancake batter that was so thick and gooey I knew it would never flip on a frying pan. Instead of throwing out the expensive batter, I closed my eyes and imagined what I could shape the batter into instead. What else do I like? Bread? No, it wouldn't rise enough. Cake? No, too much of a pain. Muffins? Hmm ... that just might work. I added a little more almond milk to my batter and found that I could thin it out enough to have a muffin-like consistency. Then I tossed in some walnuts and raisins, diced up some dried figs, sprinkled in some cinnamon and stirred it all up. I poured my batter into the muffin tins and tossed it in the oven. And guess what? What would have made lousy pancakes ended up making some pretty well-shaped—and might I add, tasty—muffins. **Point:** When you tackle any situation in a creative manner, don't expect that the outcome will be exactly what you envisioned. Sometimes, it ends up even better. ☺

It may not look good to the rest of the world, but it sure tastes good to you.

Case in point: I was at my local health food store and saw a jar of Nomato Sauce for those of us who miss tomato sauce but can't tolerate tomatoes well. I was so excited. I immediately checked out the ingredients and realized that I could easily make a similar sauce at home from scratch. I have an electrical juicer so I juiced carrots and beets. Then I added onion, garlic, lemon juice and a bunch of spices that are typically found in Italian dishes, like basil and oregano. My concoction was really watery. I needed a thickener. So I added some walnuts and threw in some carrot and beet pulp that was extracted from the juicer. I blended it all together and voilá!

Only I discovered that I used too many beets in my sauce. Instead of the reddish orange Mediterranean type of sauce I was hoping for, I ended up with a magenta psychedelic sauce that dyed my rice pasta noodles hot pink (e-mail maria@campuscalm.com if you want me to send you a photo). But here's the thing: it tasted really good. So good that I took my invention to my parents' house. My dad laughed at my pink pasta but decided to take a bite. He admitted that it actually tasted great. **Point:** Sometimes, what hatches from the creative process isn't welcomed by society at large. We have two choices: 1) Educate them on the value of our new creation … or in my case, have them taste it. 2) Accept that you will be one of few who enjoy your brilliance and so what? I'll enjoy my hot pink pasta all by myself, thank you very much.

Accept being the meatball on top of a sea of spaghetti.
When you commit to creative thinking, you are committing to heading down crooked counter-paths while society at large tiptoes down the straight and narrow path that is clearly laid out for us. My friend Carleton Kendrick says, "Creativity often takes a form that challenges, because if you are coming forth through the creative effort that is going to counter, question or totally turn on its head or on its side a prevailing viewpoint, cultural belief or dictum, that is scary to most people."

When you choose to not play by all of society's rules, you will be met with resistance. People will not "get you." When I arrive at family parties, I'm always the oddball who brings my own gluten-free, dairy-free food instead of munching away at the awesome-looking taco dip on the table. At wedding showers, I endure the stares when I pass by the dessert table. I hear other women whisper, "Oohhh, that's why she's sooo thin." When I say "No thank you" to the cake, I get asked, "Are you still on that diet?" **Point:** Society fears divergence from the norm. So if you're going to think differently, prepare yourself to sometimes be treated differently. Be prepared to trust and respect yourself more, too, though, because that's an added bonus of freeing yourself to the creative process. When someone asks me if I'm still on that diet, I respond, "Yes, and I will be for the rest of my life. And I'm loving every second of it."

> ⑥ ⑥
> If you're going to think differently, prepare yourself to sometimes be treated differently. Be prepared to trust and respect yourself more, too, though, because that's an added bonus of freeing yourself to the creative process.
> ⑥ ⑥ ⑥

Want to join me at the creative thinker's table? Great, I'll bring the muffins. ☺

⑥ ⑥ ⑥

Tap Your Inner Picasso. Be Marketable No Matter What Your College Major ...

Creativity suffers when it is used solely as a means to secure a job or to create a product in order to make money. That being said, your ability to conceive of fresh ideas makes you marketable no matter what your college major or what line of work you choose to try out. I had the opportunity to chat with a few employers about how creativity makes interns and new graduates desirable job candidates in all fields. Listen to the employers who hire college graduates like you.

Creativity is one of the most important skills that we look for in prospective employees. Competition in the media industry continues to get more intense, so at the TV station and newspaper that I work for we don't want to tell the same stories, sell the same advertising packages or create the same promotional campaigns as our competitors. We want to do things that are unique and that will give us an advantage over other media outlets. Whether in our newsroom or our sales force, building a team of people who have creative and innovative ideas is critical to our long-term success, particularly as the industry continues to evolve in response to new technologies.

Monica Egert Smith, Senior Director/Community Service, The Dallas Morning News/WFAA-TV

In the practice of law, young lawyers spend hours upon hours researching through "dusty" old legal opinions. Even though most of this work is now performed online, these young lawyers can become disillusioned or lulled into complacency, believing that it's all been done before and there are no original ideas or fact scenarios.

*A lawyer's weapon is the argument, and the very nature
of argument is creativity. An honest appraisal of the law
is always required and sometimes leads to a legal dead
end for the client. Instead of merely pointing out that dead
end and calling it a day, the tenacious and creative young
lawyer will offer one or more alternative routes (perhaps not
even through the legal system) that may allow the clients to
achieve their goals or portions thereof. When young lawyers
realize that helping their clients succeed is their measure
of success, the law is no longer the chains that bind, but
rather a framework within which their creativity can be
unleashed.*

Thomas R. Stauch, Nowak & Stauch, LLP

Create for the Sake of Creation

Even though I want you to see that creativity can make you market-able in today's ever-changing job market, your willingness to be cre-ative can also help you find the kind of personal contentment that no amount of money could ever measure. As Alexandra Levit, Campus Calm's Twentysomething Career Expert, shows creativity is about loving every second as the magic of your mind unfolds.

Writing Creatively for the Love of the Process
By Alexandra Levit, Twentysomething Career Expert, Campus Calm

I'm known for being a nonfiction author. I have three published books in the career advice space, and another on the way. I also have a business blog called Water Cooler Wisdom and write for the career sections of several major Websites. A few years ago, I had the opportunity to do a nationally syndicated advice column for Tribune Media Services, and my goal is to someday be a print columnist for the *New York Times*.

But once upon a time, I wanted to be a novelist. I wrote my first young adult novel, Peter's Friends, when I was in high school, and my dad had it published with a small press during my freshman year of college. I sold all 500 copies.

When I graduated, it was really important to my father that I establish myself in a field where I could learn marketable skills, so I started a job as an account coordinator for a top public relations agency in New York. But I never forgot about writing fiction, and on the weekends when I wasn't working, I finished a new novel about the lives of teenage celebrities.

I set my mind to finding a literary agent as soon as the book was done, and much to my surprise, I attracted the attention of a prestigious one relatively easily. I thought that my battle to get my fiction published was over at the age of 24, but it wasn't. The book received excellent feedback from several editors and even the producers at a major cable network, but no one bought it. I was devastated.

Once I realized I wasn't going to be published any time soon, I stopped writing fiction for a while. I found, though, that my life was empty without creative writing. Slowly but surely, I picked it up again—at first just in the form of journal entries. Now, a few years later, I've started working on an autobiographical piece about growing up in a troubled family. Because I now have a professional image to uphold, I am not sure this story can ever be published even if I have the opportunity. Except funnily enough, I don't care. I've learned to embrace the creative process for the process' sake.

Many people want to be creative writers, but doing it for the right reasons and going about it in the most productive way are a different story. When I was in college, I wish someone had shared this advice:

Be confident that you have something to say.
Maybe you're thinking, "What makes me qualified to write the great American novel? There are plenty of people out there who are better writers than I am." This may be true, but none of them have lived your life or have your perspective on the world—which brings me to my next point.

Be true to your experiences.
Write what you feel passionately about, not what you think other people want to read. If you try to be someone you're not, your creative product will suffer for it. How do you know when you're being authentic? Your words will flow easily, and it won't seem like work.

> "Write what you feel passionately about, not what you think other people want to read."
> -Alexandra Levit

Do it for yourself, not for the fame.
A lot of people write fiction because they crave the fame that comes with a bestselling novel. Remember than less than 1 percent of writers ever achieve this status, and as a whole, the creative writing world is notoriously difficult to break into and doesn't pay that well once you do. So if you want to do it, do it because you love it and because it infuses your life with meaning, not because of what or where you think it will get you.

Put in the time.
My mother used to say that anything worth doing requires effort, and the same goes for good writing. Even naturally talented writers have to hone their craft, so read books, take classes, let your family and friends critique your work. And practice. Writing every day will eventually result in something publishable.

Keep your day job.
The days of starving for your art are over. Recognize that you can still be a strong creative writer while succeeding at a job that pays your bills. You can also find ways to be creative in your daily working life, like identifying a problem in the organization that you can design a unique solution to fix.

© *2008-2009 Alexandra Levit*

Need some extra help with finding ways to be more creative? I have a few final suggestions.

Do:

◉ daydream more and not just about the cute guy or girl in Psych 101. Imagine the kind of world you want to live in, and then use your unique strengths to work to help create it;

◉ look at a problem and think of an unusual way to solve it. Did you know that the average adult thinks of 3-6 alternatives for any given situation? The average child thinks of 60. So hang out with some kids and tap into their creativity!

Don't:

◉ ever be afraid to voice a dissenting opinion. The rest of the world isn't always going to agree with you, nor should it. But if you believe that something is right in your heart, hold true to it because chances are there are a lot of other people out there who feel the same way and are just too scared to say it out loud;

◉ ever accept an answer to a question that doesn't feel right in your gut. Practice trusting your intuition more.

Everything I've been talking about so far requires that you know yourself pretty well and that you know your values, your beliefs, the things that make you authentically you. If you want some motivation to focus inward, keep reading.

" **Look inside. That way lies dancing to the melodies spun out by your own heart.** "

– Anna Quindlen

6 | Focus Inward

If you could forget for one minute what your friends demand, your teachers require and your parents expect of you, what would you want for yourself? What picture of success do you envision that would make you happy? Do you want to wear a pin-striped suit to the office and joke around the water cooler? Do you want to interact with people every day over power lunches and have a corner office with a great view? Or would you rather plant yourself under a tree and write a book? Have you ever taken the time to ask yourself these types of questions?

Wrap your mind around your unique picture of success. What does it feel like? Look like? Sound like? Freeze that picture in your mind and work to achieve it. Don't be afraid to change that picture of success, though, as you grow and learn new things. Being brave enough to change directions based on new information and experiences will help to determine your future success and happiness.

Let's say you graduate from college and you find a job in your field with a starting salary of $35,000. Your best friend in a completely different field lands a job that starts at $50,000. Does the difference in salaries bother you? If you took the time to get to know yourself really well and assess your values and the kind of life you want to lead, you'll be in a better position to congratulate your friend and be happy for her than to succumb to jealousy or feeling like you're less successful by comparison. Make sense?

Students' Self-image Secrets Revealed

Students, do you want to learn about a free, 15-minute exercise that will help you discover your unique, authentic self? Read on.

Until a few years ago, I had no idea who I was without my achievements. My career goals—they were my LIFE goals. They were all I thought about, 24/7. Showing the world. Making others proud of me. My portfolio. My résumé. My perfect GPA—that was how I measured my self-worth.

Can any of you relate? If you're not getting good grades, working or volunteering, winning awards or planning for your future, do you know who you are? Dr. Nathaniel Branden*, psychotherapist and expert on the psychology of self-esteem, says, "The tragedy is that so many people look for self-confidence and self-respect everywhere ex-

---

* *Nathaniel, Branden, PhD.* How to Raise Your Self-Esteem: The Proven Action-Oriented Approach to Greater Self-Respect and Self-Confidence. *(Bantam Books, 1987), 9.*

cept within themselves, and so they fail in their search." Dr. Branden was right: my résumé, though impressive, didn't fill me up inside.

After 26 years, I decided to find my authentic self. I sat down with pen and paper and proceeded to list exactly who I was without my achievements. Some ideas came easily and others did not. If you struggle to come up with a few, don't worry. Ask a trusted friend or family member to help you out. Return the favor by telling her why she's so great, with or without her accomplishments.

So, who am I?

I am ...

- a person who has a big heart;

- a person who finds satisfaction in helping others feel good about themselves;

- a person who loves her family and wants to spend time with them;

- a woman who is lucky enough to have a fantastic, supportive and loving husband who is truly my best friend (we've been together since high school);

- a person who seeks meaning in the world;

- a kid at heart who needs to remember my roots (I recently bought a bicycle and rediscovered the exhilaration of pedaling the evening and my cares away);

- a physical being who loves to dance, bike, rollerblade, jump rope and hike in the woods;

◎ a person who loves nature—minus the bugs!

◎ a person who feels a sense of calm every time I sit by the water;

◎ a person who will laugh at just about any joke and make just about anyone feel funny;

◎ a principled writer who believes in the power to earn a good living while doing something positive for society;

◎ a woman who is flawed and has doubts but continues to love herself anyway.

All these things make up who I am authentically. They will never change no matter what mistakes I make, what "failures" I endure or what success I achieve. Now that you've read through my exercise in self-love, give it a try! I promise you that it'll be the most fulfilling exercise you've ever completed.

Check out: **www.campuscalm.com/selfimage**

If you need further inspiration to begin looking inward to shape your self-identity, listen to the words of Christine Hassler, Campus Calm's Twentysomething Survival Expert. A life coach and twentysomething crisis survivor, Christine's latest book is called *The 20-Something Manifesto: Quarter-Lifers Speak Out about Who They Are, What They Want, and How to Get It.*

Discover Who You Are Before Deciding What You Want
By: Christine Hassler, Twentysomething Survival Expert, Campus Calm

Growing up and even through high school and college I was never one to listen to myself. To be honest, I never knew how. It was hard to learn how to do, especially when most of my life was spent listening to all of the expectations I had of myself or the expectations I thought others had of me. Fitting in was an important part of my life; I focused on looking the part I thought I should play. When it came time to make that all-important decision about college, I did what I thought I was supposed to do and graduated in 3½ years with a double major, three internships under my belt and a résumé jampacked with extracurricular activities. And, oh, I had a 3.9 GPA too.

Before the ink on my diploma was dry, I hightailed it to Los Angeles to pursue what I thought was my dream of working in the entertainment industry. The funny thing was, I had no clue what I wanted to do but trusted the idea that once I set sight on the place where my life would begin, everything would fall into place. I paid my dues (working 12-hour days for $400 a week) and went from one job to the next until I landed a position as a literary agent at a very prestigious entertainment company. Along with a real salary, I had an office with a view, an assistant, business cards, power lunches and clients. I attended industry events and started dating. From the outside, my life looked great, and I was well on my way to achieving everything I thought I was supposed to. There was only one major problem: I was completely and utterly miserable.

Even though I tried to like my job, I didn't last much longer at the career I thought I wanted. The long hours, cutthroat competition and rude people (even I was becoming one of them!) were making getting up every day painful. I was suffering from migraines nearly every day. Constant feelings of stress and frustration, coupled with too much caffeine and artificial sweeteners, threw my hormones and immune system completely out of whack. So I quit—with no real backup plan. I didn't have Plan B because Plan A was supposed to work. I was terrified, but I knew this job wasn't right for me. Leaving it fixed all my woes, temporarily. Soon the same feelings of depression, confusion and angst set back in.

The next couple of years can only be described as a never-ending roller coaster of events complete with twists and turns I never thought imaginable. I went into debt, got diagnosed with an autoimmune disorder, had a major blowup with my family where my mother and I did not speak for months and got dumped by my fiancé six months before my wedding.

I came to a point in my life where I had a choice to make. I could continue the particular ride I was on, or I could jump off and start listening to who I was, not who I was told to be, and what I wanted, not what others thought I should want or what I thought I should want. When I started not only to listen to but also to trust my inner self, life started to fall into place and things started to make sense as I used this time to carve out my own identity. I stopped relying on the many images and ideals floating around that were telling me who I should be. I realized that no one knows me better than, well, me! I just had never gotten off the treadmill of overachieving and living in the future to stop and figure ME out.

It's funny that some of the things I endured—the grueling years at college, the move to Los Angeles and the overwhelmingly stressful career—helped shape me to become a voice of encouragement and support for men and women experiencing what I've come to call a twenty-something crisis. My experiences became the inspiration for my first book, *Twenty-Something, Twenty-Everything* and also inspired me to become a life coach dedicated to transforming the twentysomething experience.

Many of my clients often talk about the difficulty in trusting their inner compass. They're afraid it will steer them on an even worse path than the one they're currently on. From birth, we all learn to take clues about how to act (or not act) from individuals we observe at home, school, work or in public. Often we see as our only choice to model ourselves on what we see in others. We adopt certain characteristics in order to fit in or be accepted. This becomes risky behavior when we start to reflect our outside circumstances and not allow our true, inner-self to emerge. With all this focus on others' actions, it's no wonder we have such a difficult time trusting ourselves.

One major consequence with modeling our thoughts and behaviors after others is that we end up traveling down their life's path and not our own. I wrote my second book, *The 20 Something Manifesto* after spending five years coaching and researching twentysomethings and seeing the need to redefine what this decade is really about. It's important to realize and accept that our paths and experiences are supposed to be different. Rather than compare ourselves to others, our direction should come from inside. Once I started listening to myself and making my own choices, I was able to head down the path that was meant for me. If I had allowed my experiences to paralyze me, rather than trust my gut and learn from those experiences, I wouldn't be leading a happy, successful and purpose-driven[*] life.

---

[*] *Term borrowed from Rick Warren's bestselling book* The Purpose Driven Life.

It's hard to trust yourself. It took me years to be able to have confidence that I was headed in the right direction. I encourage twenty-somethings to build your self-trust muscle by making decisions on your own, without consulting anyone else! I learned if I listened to things like, "Why don't you do this," or "I think you would be better off if you did this," in the end, I would doubt my decisions, which would make me even more frustrated.

> "You don't have to take the unsolicited advice loved ones may be throwing your way. 'Thanks for your opinion,' is an appropriate and empowering response!"
>
> -Christine Hassler

Advice is defined as "an opinion or recommendation offered as a guide to action," with the key word here being *opinion*. Remember, everyone has opinions and there's no law against sharing them. You don't have to take the unsolicited advice loved ones may be throwing your way. "Thanks for your opinion," is an appropriate and empowering response! What we do with the advice or opinions given is completely up to us. When I recognized that, I no longer doubted my own decisions. I just listened to what was said, thanked the person speaking and then continued to listen to my gut. It has yet to steer me wrong.

It takes time to learn how to direct your own path in this world. With so many influences surrounding us, it's no wonder we all struggle with finding confidence in ourselves. Have faith that you too can get to a place where you'll no longer let outside things dictate your thought patterns and actions. Instead, you'll be able not only to recognize that you have an inner compass, but also to allow it to steer you in a direction that's meant for no one but you.

© 2008-2009 Christine Hassler

—— ⑥ ⑥ ⑥ ——

Ever wonder how some people seem to glow with an inner confidence and contentment? They just seem so secure with who they are and they appear to know themselves really, really well.

What about you? Do you know yourself, inside and out? Do you know your life goals?

Q: "Jeez, Maria, how am I supposed to have clearly defined life goals at age 16? Or 18, 20 or 23 years old for that matter?"

A: Chill! When focusing inward, you'll stress less when you realize that you're going to change your mind about your life goals MANY times throughout your life and that's totally okay. In fact, it's okay to not have life goals at all. Instead, think short-term goals because this process will help you focus in the present. Sure, everyone has a few things that they want to do before they die (climb Mount Everest, sail the world, bungee jump off The Empire State Building ☺) but the idea of a life goal seems pretty intimidating, huh? When I first got out of college and went on job interviews, people in drabby gray pin-striped suits kept asking me questions like, "Where do you see yourself in five years? What do you envision your life to be like in 10 years?" I wanted to respond, "How the heck should I know? I don't even know if I want this job I'm interviewing for today!"

I hated those questions because I couldn't answer them. I honestly didn't know the answers.

Today, I'm totally cool with the fact that I don't have my life mapped out ... and I'm 30 (the horror!). I know where I want to journey with Campus Calm this year and the year after that but I don't know where I see my life or my business in five or 10 years. That doesn't mean I don't have long-term personal goals or business goals. I want to write more books like this one; I want to produce a line of exercise DVDs for students; I want to establish a scholarship fund for kids who celebrate good health, happiness and the pursuit of knowledge over the almighty grade. I want to dip my toe in the Pacific Ocean; I want to hula dance in Maui; I even want to gaze up at the Sistine Chapel in Italy. I want to grow old with my husband; I might want to have kids someday ... or I might not. Oh yeah, and I want to slip my feet into a pair of high-heeled tap shoes and reunite with my long-lost love of professional (or should I say amateur) tap dancing.

Maybe all these goals on my list will materialize and maybe they won't. Being okay with not knowing, not always needing to have the answers all the time is totally liberating.

Why don't you try it yourself and see?

If you want to download and print a larger copy of the "Unlock Your Goals & Values" exercise, visit: **www.campuscalm.com/book/exercises**

Unlock Your Goals & Values: It all begins with Y-O-U

Campus Calm believes that the key to unlocking your present and future goals and values starts with your ability to turn your attention inward and REALLY listen to your own voice. Sometimes if we're searching for answers, we simply need to ask ourselves thought-provoking questions. The following questions will help get you started on your path to self-discovery. I've even answered a few myself to help break the ice.

What am I most proud of?

◎ I am proud of the fact that I can – <u>use my unique skills to help others and earn a living</u>.

◎ I am proud of the way that I – <u>never give up on my dreams, even when things get hard</u>.

◎ I am proud of how I treat – <u>myself with the same compassion that I extend to those I love</u>.

◎ I am proud of how I love – <u>all parts of myself, especially my quirks</u>.

◎ I am proud of my inner – <u>resilience because it took me a long long time to find it</u>.

How do I define success?

⊚ I am successful if I – <u>do right by my values</u>.

⊚ I am successful if I can earn – <u>the financial means necessary to have choices and control my own destiny</u>.

⊚ I am successful if I live life – <u>by my own terms</u>.

⊚ I am successful if I respect – <u>my own dreams and invest in my self-growth</u>.

⊚ I am successful if I give – <u>my talents to the world in a way that's inspiring and meaningful</u>.

⊚ I want to be remembered by – <u>the many ways I loved others while I was on this planet</u>.

Okay, now it's your turn to focus inward.

Who am I?

⊚ I am a person who seeks meaning in _____

_____

⊚ I am a person who finds satisfaction in_____

_____

⊚ I am a person who loves _____

_____

◉ I am a person who is lucky enough to _____

_____

◉ I am a person who feels a sense of calm each time I _____

_____

Which is more important, the degree or the education?

◉ I believe being educated means_____

_____

◉ I believe an education enables me to do _____

_____

◉ I believe an education never stops _____

_____

◉ I believe learning should be_____

_____

◉ I believe grades measure _____ . However, no letter
  grade could possibly measure _____

_____

◉ I believe an education is the key to _____

_____

◉ If I weren't in college right now, I'd be _____

_____

What do I think makes for a successful life?

⊚ I believe I will be successful when _____

_____

⊚ I believe I will be successful if _____

_____

⊚ I believe I can't be successful without _____

_____

⊚ I believe my ability to be successful resides within_____

_____

⊚ I believe successful people love _____

_____

⊚ I believe successful people know how to _____

_____

What do I think makes me a good person?

⊚ I like myself when I _____

_____

⊚ I think I am a good person because I _____

_____

🌀 I think my good _____

_____ make(s) me unique.

🌀 I think I am a good person despite my _____

_____

🌀 My most imperfectly perfect quality is _____

_____

What are my values?

🌀 I am responsible when _____

_____

🌀 I believe all people deserve _____

_____

🌀 I feel empowered by my ability to _____

_____

🌀 I value myself when _____

_____

🌀 I respect others when _____

_____

Career exploration: What experiences will make *me* happy and fulfilled?*

◎ I am most happy when I am _____

_____

◎ I am good at _____

_____ ("Nothing" doesn't count

☺). Ask a friend, relative or teacher for help if you don't know.

◎ The following things come easily to me: _____

_____

_____

◎ A career in _____ sounds interesting to me.

◎ I want a job that enables me to _____

_____

◎ I don't want a position where I would have to _____

_____

_____

◎ I want an experience that enables me to use these skills: _____

_____

_____

_____

* *Campus Calm believes that the heart of any successful career search is Y-O-U. While you can respect others' opinions, your friends, teachers and parents aren't going to shadow you to work for the next 40 years. So why would you allow them to dictate one of the biggest decisions of your life?*

⑨ I want a job that enables me to enjoy this kind of lifestyle: _____

_____

_____

_____

Post your answers on the Campus Calm forum: **www.campuscalm. com/forum** and connect with other students. Bounce your ideas off one another and learn. Take the best ideas that seem right for you and write them down. Remember that not everything on your list will materialize into a job. That's cool. That is what a personal life is for, after all. But if you're feeling stuck when it comes to connecting your goals, values and passions with jobs that may be a good fit, it's time to get some help. I suggest that you make an appointment to visit your college career center and get some help from a trained career counselor. A trained professional can help you flesh out and— ultimately—take the baby steps necessary to find a career path that's uniquely right for you.

Do:

◉ sit down and make a list of all the pastimes that bring you joy. Then find ways to make more time for them! Or what about turning your pastime into a job—get paid for what you love to do;

◉ remember to say: it's MY life! Repeat this affirmation: Before I say "yes" (again) to something or someone, I will ask myself, "Is this new task in alignment with my goals? Will saying 'yes' make me happy? Do I have time to add another thing to my schedule? What will I have to sacrifice if I say 'yes' to this new activity?" Be honest and don't be afraid to put your own needs first every now and then.

Don't:

◉ spend so much time listening to everyone else's opinions about your own life that you forget to let the most important person weigh in ... YOU!

How I Focused Inward to Find the Right College Major ... and You Can Too!
By: Kristen Szustakowski, Editorial Intern, Campus Calm

My name is Kristen, and I am a happy college student.

Part of what makes me such a happy college student is that I *heart* my major. But it took me a long time to figure out what it is that I hearted. I wasn't one of those kids who knew what they wanted to do at age five and have been heading in that direction ever since. I wasn't even one of those kids who had it narrowed down to a few choices upon entering college. Nope, I was one of those indecisive individuals who walked onto campus with nine potential futures floating around in my head. I have had as many different majors as I have lost college ID cards: three. It took a lot of "focusing inward," a term I've borrowed from Maria, before I was able to make the choice of becoming the happy English major I am today.

At my freshman orientation at SUNY Fredonia, I remember standing under the hot July sun in a circle with a collection of other nervous new students. We were asked to do what many find torturous: introduce ourselves to the group we'd be spending the next two days with. As I listened to everyone talk about dreams of pursuing their love for music and teaching (the two most popular majors at Fredonia), I thought about what I could say. When my turn came up, I said, "Hi, my name is Kristen. I'm from West Seneca, New York and I'm majoring in ... criminal justice."

That last part was a lie. My major was "liberal arts," a.k.a. "undecided." Criminal justice happened to be the flavor of the week. I was just too ashamed to say I was entering college without knowing exactly what I wanted to do with my life. In my head, the conversation would go like this:

"What are you majoring in?"

"I'm undecided."

"Then ... why are you even here?"

Of course I ended up feeling like a tool when we had to separate into groups based on our majors and everyone realized I was only playing the part of a student who knew where her life was going.

The problem was, I had it ingrained in my head that *undeclared, undecided* and *liberal arts* were all polite ways of saying a person was lazy, confused and uninterested in anything life has to offer. I didn't want to be labeled any of those things. The reason I hadn't chosen a major yet was because I wanted to do everything. I couldn't limit myself to one passion. So I lied about having a major, hoping that maybe the other college freshmen would take me more seriously.

As I got further into my first semester, my liberal arts friends began to vanish into orbs of business, visual arts and history. I became more uncomfortable without a defined path. So uncomfortable that one night toward the end of my first semester, I locked myself in my dorm room and refused to leave until I chose something. I took a seat on my yellow and blue blanketed bed with my college catalogue. By two in the morning, I decided on English adolescence education. I figured I had been writing my whole life, and the only practical thing a writer can do is teach. High school was fun, so why not? I called my dad the next day to tell him that I not only had decided on a major, I declared one and was now signing up for the appropriate classes.

"That was a little quick," my dad commented over the phone. His voice made me nervous and I hoped that my impulsive decision was the right one.

I was reassured when I began taking Novels and Tales, World Poetry and English Composition. I couldn't believe reading short stories and writing narratives counted as homework! I love that kind of stuff! It wasn't until the first semester of my junior year that I began taking more education classes. Suddenly I wasn't so sure about the major I had chosen. People began asking why I had chosen to become a teacher, and when my response was, "I need a way to make money while I write," I realized I had gotten into education for the wrong reasons. I started feeling guilty going to class because everyone around me was there for the right ones.

One warm October day, I sat across from the sixth grader I was supposed to be tutoring. His vocabulary test sat on the table between us. He had his arms crossed in front of him and he was taking turns glaring at both me and his paper.

"I'd rather be outside," he said. I looked around at the blue tile walls of the middle school library and thought, "Me too." That day I realized I absolutely could not be a teacher. I prepared myself to tell my parents the big news.

I waited until my entire family sat down to lunch the following weekend. My parents talked about their jobs. My sister talked about her classes. When there was a break in conversation, I just decided to have out with it, preparing myself for a whack on the head from the newspaper my dad had sitting next to him.

"I don't want to be a teacher," I said, bracing myself for them to react.

"We were wondering when you were going to realize that," Dad said. Mom agreed. My jaw dropped.

As I started telling my friends and teachers I was dropping the education program, I got mixed reactions. Many were not the least bit surprised with my decision. They encouraged me to discover what it was I truly loved. Others became angry with me and insisted I was making a tremendous mistake. I was getting mixed up and confused. I began second guessing myself. Maybe my dislike for teaching was simply a phase. Everyone has a point in their college careers where they hate their major, but it passes. But then why wasn't mine passing?

Finally, I realized this was a decision only I could make. It was my life. What my friends said and what my professors said didn't matter. I began analyzing my classes over the past few years, dissecting what it was that kept me in English adolescence education for so long, and what it was that had turned me off. The conclusion I finally arrived at was so simple: I like to write. English kept me in that major; teaching pushed me out. I felt like I knew that all along, and if I hadn't been so uncomfortable being undeclared my freshman year, if I had taken more time to feel out my major choice instead of jumping right in, I probably would have declared English from the start.

I realize now that there is nothing wrong with being undeclared. In fact, it's good to be undeclared. There is no reason anyone should feel like they have to enter college knowing exactly what they want to be when they grow up. I don't know why I thought I needed a path set in stone, because if there's one thing I've learned, life is never set in stone. Being undeclared provides the opportunity to focus inward, to dig out those dreams you've let gather dust over the years, to brush them off and replace them in your heart. Those dreams and those passions have made me (and hopefully will make you) that happy college student.

"It's good to be undeclared. There is no reason anyone should feel like they have to enter college knowing exactly what they want to be when they grow up."

-Kristen Szustakowski

" The finest gift you can give anyone is encouragement. "

– Sidney Madwed

7 | Surround Yourself with Positive People

If you want to develop your inner strength, surrounding yourself with people who glow from the inside out is the way to do it. People who love their lives and take pride in living each day to the fullest. If your family wants you to be happy and successful on your own terms (see Q&A on the following page), turn to them for support. If your friends lift you up, make it a priority to spend quality time with them.

Can't find anyone who "gets" the authentic you? Go out there and find a support network. While you're busy having fun and making new friends, watch how quickly your own self-confidence begins to soar! I speak from experience. Reaching out to other writers and creative types was the most inspiring thing I've ever done and Campus Calm would not exist if I didn't have those people in my life to encourage my dreams*.

Q: "How can I talk to my parents about my goals when they are so negative and keep trying to steer me down their clearly-constructed boring path instead?"

A: Communication is like playing catch—it needs to be received. The best time to share your goals with your parents is when you've first acknowledged their communication to you. Keep in mind that you need not agree with their dreams for you in order to acknowledge them. You can say something like, "I know you love me very much and want me to (fill in the blank). You want me to be successful and so do I. Now that I've heard your ideas for me, I'd like to share with you what I'm passionate about."

Parents want their kids to be happy, but they also want them to have a plan. If you know what your strengths are—the ones that make your heart sing—and you've done the necessary research and planning to double-check your career goals, then your parents are more likely to back off. Once you've completed your reality check, start taking steps right now to begin living your dreams, and forget about fulfilling your parents' fantasies about your future.

Answer courtesy of Barbara McRae, MCC, Teen Parenting Expert, Campus Calm

---

* In Chapter 6, I cautioned you about listening to people who were not supportive of your goals and dreams and recommended that you politely hear them out but not necessarily follow their advice. What I'm telling you now doesn't contradict that message because I'm talking about actively finding a support network. You surround yourself with these positive people because you know they'll help you figure out how to achieve your goals. They want for you what you want for you and they believe you can achieve it.

Pardon me, I believe you have a positive aura. I can feel it!

This might seem like a no-brainer, but have you ever wondered what characteristics positive people share? If you were asked to describe a positive person, what would you say? That they smile more than they scowl? Laugh more than they grunt? Sing more than they sigh? See the glass as half full—yeah, I'm sick to death of that analogy too, but I bet you were also thinking it.

Sure, someone who is high on life 24/7 is kind of annoying (and may actually be high on something other than life ☺), but genuinely positive people are a magnet. You want to be around them. Your day is brightened by their presence.

Characteristics That Distinguish Positive People

Honesty. There are those people who will tell you what you want to hear. Then there are truly positive people who are brave enough to be honest with you, while still being supportive and having a positive attitude.

Impractically practical. Positive people will listen to your wacky improbable dream to, say, direct and distribute your own documentary films. They'll respond with, "Why not?" They have a can-do attitude about even the seemingly most difficult things. But a truly helpful positive person will encourage you to look at the practical steps you must take in order to realize the most grandiose dream. Even if they don't know what those steps are, they will encourage you to surround yourself with people who do.

Generous. Positive people are entitled to a bad day once in a while. Their car stalls, their laptop breaks, the dog eats the napkin with their new crush's phone number. Positive people are even allowed to occasionally curse their decision to get out of bed in the morning. But if you have some exciting news to share, positive people can put their complaints aside long enough to share in your happiness for a while. They do this because they care about you. But they also realize that your positive energy may actually rub off on them, bringing sunshine to their otherwise gray day.

Internally driven. Positive people recognize that positivity is a personal choice. They realize that when they choose to see the gems life has to offer instead of the grime, they will be happier, healthier and more satisfied for it. Positive people choose to be resilient and then learn how to craft the tools that will allow them to live the life they desire.

> Positive people realize that when they choose to see the gems life has to offer instead of the grime, they will be happier, healthier and more satisfied for it.

Did I miss any characteristics? What do you think distinguishes a positive person? Write down your answer in the space provided below. Consider posting it on the Campus Calm forum: **www.campuscalm.com/forum**.

12 Ways to Surround Yourself with Positive People

1. Join clubs on campus and make new friends with positive, happy people. Find the one person in the room who can't stop smiling, and feed off his or her energy.

2. Join a professional organization. You don't have to wait for your diploma to network and learn from working professionals in your field. Many organizations have special member discounts for students. Take advantage of them! A word to the wise: don't join an organization just to put it on your résumé. If you're going to join, be an active member. Network with other professionals and learn more about specific careers that sound exciting to you.

3. Take advantage of internship opportunities. Besides the obvious learning opportunities and résumé builders, internships are a great way to surround yourself with positive people who share your interests. Make friends with other interns. Make a pact to learn from one another and help each other instead of competing. Then enjoy the rewards of teamwork and friendship for the rest of your life.

Case in point: when I was 24, I befriended another writer. We were kindred wordsmiths who clicked from "Hello." However, we were both still a little insecure, so we let things like intimidation, jealousy and competition dampen our friendship. Five years later, we're in a much healthier place, able to cheer each other's writing successes without feeling *less than* by comparison. We're both thrilled that we've been able to reconnect. But look at the time and support we missed in between. I consider it a waste.

4. Visit your campus career center. My college career counselor was my life coach through college and my first two years out of school. I was SO LUCKY to have her, but it wasn't just luck. I had something to do with it because I made the choice to walk through my career center's doors. Your career counselor can be your biggest cheerleader as you navigate college and transition into the working world. But you have to be the one to make the first appointment.

5. If you're lucky enough to come from a family of positive thinkers, learn from them. Pick one or two family members you admire and interview them. Ask them how they've come to view life so positively and ask them what their secret to happiness and success is.

6. Google "positive people" and "positive thinkers." What did you come up with?

7. Start a Positive Thinking blog.

8. Write a research paper about what makes people resilient. Don't just go to your library, though, and pull together second-hand information. Get out there and do some primary research. Interview people in your community who have overcome hardship and who maintain a positive attitude.*

---

* *Tip generated from Dr. Al Siebert, author of* The Resiliency Advantage.

9. Give back to others. Be a positive-thinking role model for your friends. If you're a positive thinker, you'll naturally attract other positive thinkers into your life.

10. Make friends with happy students you admire. Campus Calm's Body Image Expert, Courtney E. Martin, used to write letters to girls she had a "crush" on. She'd tell them why she thought they were awesome and then she'd invite them to hang out. According to a 2009 mtvU study of over 2,200 college students, 77 percent of students reported that they turn to friends for help when they're in emotional distress. Wouldn't you like an established support network of positive friends to turn to?

11. Learn from enthusiastic professors. Heard of a funny professor on campus who's great at engaging students? Maybe one who's awesome at stirring his class up in heated debate. Check out his classes when your next semester's course catalogue comes out. Make it a point to take classes from professors who love teaching and who are a joy to be around. Learning shouldn't be boring. If a teacher loves his job, his enthusiasm will shine through and he'll be a better teacher and role model for you.

12. Find a boss who is willing to be your mentor. I know, I know, you have to find a job first, and as a brand new graduate, shouldn't your main objective be to make yourself look irresistible to employers regardless of what you want out of the deal? Well, yes and no.

Yes, as a new graduate you have to be willing to work extra hard to find a job, and you have to realize that you're not necessarily going to find your dream job right away, and that's okay. That being said, you

Ask your potential bosses if they like working with new graduates. Find out if they're willing to mentor you if you do a great job for them in return.

have a college education and you bring passion, skills and enthusiasm to an employer, so why not use the interview process as a way for you to ask some questions too? Ask your potential bosses if they like working with new graduates. Why or why not? Find out if they're willing to mentor you if you do a great job for them in return.

When I went for my first job at *The Buffalo News*, I wanted to be a features reporter. I ended up as an advertising copywriter. Do I regret it? Absolutely not. For one thing, I learned how to write great advertising copy, which serves me well as an entrepreneur today. More importantly though, I was blessed to have an amazing first boss at *The Buffalo News*. Joe Kirchmyer, senior creative services manager, was a mentor to me in every sense of the word. He pushed for me to attend the American Society of Journalists and Authors conference in New York City when I told him I wanted to go to enhance my freelance writing career; he edited my work and gave me fantastic feedback; and he was there to answer my questions whenever I barged into his office with my business or life crisis of the moment (I was a little bit of a drama queen back then).

Salary, perks and benefits packages are all important, but finding a boss who is willing to mentor you is more important for your first couple of jobs post-graduation.

Leverage Other Positive People's Strengths

The cool part about surrounding yourself with positive people is that you can all tap into each other's strengths. In school, we so often focus on our deficits instead of celebrating the positive. When you get your report card and realize that you were excellent in three subjects and average in two, how often do you worry about the two less-than-stellar grades instead of celebrating what you're excelling in?

True innovators realize that success happens when you focus on your strengths and fill in the gaps by leveraging* other people's strengths. We give ourselves permission to stop trying to be great at everything. Take this book, for example. I love writing prose, but I'm not well-versed on the intricacies of grammar and the *many* rules of style. Granted, I know the difference between *there, their,* and *they're.* If you e-mail me with, "WHATS UP MARIA BTW I FOUND YOUR WEBSITE YOU ROCK TOTALLY ttys J.," I will probably have a coronary.

However, I know my limitations when it comes to editing. So I hired a professional editor and leveraged her strengths. I'm also not great at writing interactive quizzes. Luckily, my intern is fantastic at it! Actually, this book shows you what can happen when you surround yourself with other positive people and combine your strengths. All of my Campus Calm experts specialize in their own niche; together we provide you with the collective advice you need to stress less and transform your college experience.

So how can you and your friends leverage each other's strengths as students ... in a way that doesn't involve copying papers or cheating on an exam? ☺ Well, group projects come to mind. Maybe your group has to give an oral presentation for class. You love talking, one partner loves computer design and the other partner writes well. So you do the research together and outline the ideas. Then you present a majority of the speech, the designer designs a kick-a$$ PowerPoint

---

* *Sheri McConnell, my business coach, introduced me to the concept of leverage* www.sherimcconnell.com.

presentation and the writer writes the speech. If you all love talking, turn your presentation into a debate. My friends and I took that approach for a group presentation on TV censorship for a freshman English class, and our classmates loved it.

What else can you and your friends help each other with?

How about if it's as simple as hanging out with your friends on a Saturday night? You're the quiet one who also happens to be a great listener. Steve's the rational one who can lead some heated debates about politics, religion, energy conservation, how ridiculous old boy Hugh Hefner looks in his red velvet bathrobe (or as my husband informs me, "It's not a bathrobe, Maria. It's a smoking jacket."). ☺ Steve can engage the group for hours. Syesha's sarcastic sense of humor provides the group with comic relief when the great debate starts to get too heavy. And maybe Danny makes a lethal nacho cheese dip—because every group deserves a chef!

What if Your Current Friends Aren't Positive People?

Sometimes surrounding yourself with positive people isn't easy, especially if you've spent your life gravitating toward people who make it easy for you to give up on your ideas. If you need further motivation to find positive support, listen to the words of Ross Szabo, Campus Calm's Mental Health Survival Expert.

Finding Positive Support Starts with You
By: Ross Szabo, Mental Health Survival Expert,
Campus Calm

I speak to college students on a regular basis, and one of the most common problems I hear about is from people who want to make a positive change in their lives, but don't know how or where to begin. There's a lot of information out there about this issue and I feel like most of it makes it seem pretty easy. Once you identify that certain friends may be dragging you down, or affecting you negatively or doing anything against making you a better person, then you should just leave them. It all sounds really easy; just let them know, and go find the people or groups or other ways to help you. The reality is that people tend to have friends who validate their own negative feelings. So they usually need to change the way they feel about themselves before they're ready to ditch their old friends.

Like a lot of people, I had to learn this the hard way. When I went away to college, I brought a lot of baggage with me. At 16, I was diagnosed with bipolar disorder, and later in high school I was hospitalized for wanting to take my own life. Needless to say, I wasn't your typical college freshman, but in some ways I was just like everyone else because I thought college would be the place for me to start over. I thought I would move past all of the crap I had to deal with in high school and make the lifelong friendships I read all about from my high school graduation cards.

But how I felt about myself had a profound effect on what I did and who I hung around with in college.

When I arrived at American University, I pictured myself meeting other guys who were just like me. And I did. I made friends with people who liked to do what I did, some of which was harmless, but not all. I self-medicated by drinking as much as I could whenever I could. Unfortunately, that type of behavior is also pretty well accepted on college campuses and in some ways only upped my level of "coolness." I surrounded myself with people who saw nothing wrong with what I was doing and who helped me continue to abuse alcohol and drugs.

But self-medication can only get you so far; within two months I had a major relapse with bipolar disorder and had to take a leave of absence from college. I was hospitalized again when I got back home.

When I got out of the hospital I felt like the biggest failure in the world, like I wasn't capable of anything. I took a year off from college, often sleeping on my couch for 18 hours a day or staring out in my backyard at nothing. I developed an immense amount of self-hatred and truly felt I would be capable only of messing up important things for myself the rest of my life.

This pattern of thinking and behavior continued for another couple of years. Then I returned to American University four years after I originally started. In my first semester back I was doing okay. I tried to find people who were doing good things and not turning to partying as the only way to get through the day. But I didn't spend enough time working on my problems, and I continued to drink heavily, often when I was alone.

One night I drank more than 13 shots in an hour and then went out. I had more shots, plus beer. I passed out that night around 2 a.m.

When I woke up, my clock said 12:00, but when I looked outside it was dark. I had been passed out for 22 hours.

I looked in the mirror and I started crying. That was when I realized I couldn't continue beating myself up with all of the negative thoughts I had about myself or I would probably die. That was my rock bottom moment. You always hear about these events in peoples' lives—it's the day they changed their lives forever, just like that. If my life were a movie, the rest would have been easy. I could have just walked outside into the sunshine. Maybe a little blue bird would land on my shoulder and tell me it was going to be okay.

But in reality, the choice to turn your life around is just the beginning of a really hard process.

I really hated myself. I didn't care about finding people who cared about me or who were doing positive things, mainly because I didn't care about myself. So my first step was to learn to like myself, and that wasn't easy. I had to work hard to find one or two things I liked about myself. In times where my self-hatred would be triggered, I needed to turn to those one or two things I liked and hold on to them. Early on, I would do a lot of positive work and then have a slipup where I would go back to alcohol or other destructive things. When I woke up the next morning I would beat myself up and tell myself I couldn't change. It was then that I realized I needed to take the small positive changes I was making and move forward with them. I needed to not let my change be defined by

> "I didn't care about finding people who cared about me or who were doing positive things mainly because I didn't care about myself."
>
> -Ross Szabo

one slipup or one failure. I did all of this work with a therapist and in my first positive romantic relationship.

After I was able to do all of this work, it was a lot easier to find positive friends and people to have in my life. I know that may sound weird and it may sound even more complicated than just finding positive people to begin with, but in my experience if you don't want to see positive aspects in yourself, then finding positive people may be really challenging. Now that I've been able to surround myself with friends who care about me, I've been able to have a very healthy life. I have reconnected and furthered my friendships with a core group of guys from high school, and I've been in a romantic relationship with an amazing person who truly cares about herself, as well, for five years. If I do anything that even approaches the line of hurting myself or having thoughts of self-hatred, these people don't just let it go or encourage it. They ask me questions and let me know they care. Support from friends and significant others can mean more than anything in the world in the moments where you don't see these things in yourself.

If you're looking to make positive changes in your life, you may want to begin with thinking about yourself and what could be holding you back. If you have any thoughts of self-hatred, lack of care for yourself, or don't think you have much to offer, that may be your place to start.

Tips for Surrounding Yourself with Positive People

1. Start by looking at yourself and figuring out why you may be surrounded by negative people or people who don't care about you. If you're in a tough spot and don't care about yourself, start to think about why that's so.

2. If you do have negative thoughts about yourself, find some things you like about yourself and turn to those when you have negative thoughts. Learn to like yourself and see yourself in a positive light so you don't feel you deserve people who don't care about you.

3. Don't let any slipups or setbacks on your path to learning more about yourself define the entire journey. It's common and easy to beat yourself up when you try to make changes. Learn what you can from every situation, and have the courage to move forward.

4. After you feel good about yourself, get active and engaged to meet people. Sitting behind your computer and joining every Facebook group that interests you is different from finding some of the people in those groups and meeting them in person. Person-to-person contact is one of the most important things all people need for their brains to develop and grow.

5. Express how you feel about friends. Revealing your emotions can make you feel vulnerable, and, yes, you will run into people who don't like it. But you will develop deeper and more meaningful friendships by becoming comfortable with your emotions and letting people know where they stand in your life.

6. If you're really lost, don't give up. It can be hard to find people you get along with or people who care about you. If you're able to have one person in your life, be thankful, and hopefully you'll find ways to grow from there.

7. Consider opening communication in your family or finding a way to have members of your family understand you. Sure, your family may never "get" you, which may cause you to wonder where you came from sometimes. But unless you give your family members a chance, you'll never know what they're capable of.

"Unless you give your family members a chance, you'll never know what they're capable of."

-Ross Szabo

8. When you do have positive people in your life, don't give up on finding more. Sometimes it's easy to say you have learned enough about yourself or your friends and reach a plateau. Part of having positive influences in your life is constantly challenging yourself to grow.

© 2008-2009 Ross Szabo

———— ⓖ ⓖ ⓖ ————

Thankfully, most students don't have to learn how to persevere over adversity to the degree in which Ross did. But whether you're in a true emotional crisis or are simply looking to be proactive about infusing your life with positivity, the people you choose to surround yourself with are key.

———— ⑥ ⑥ ⑥ ————

Quiz: Am I a Supportive Friend? A Positive Thinker? Are My Friends Supportive and Positive Thinkers?

By: Kristen Szustakowski, Editorial Intern, Campus Calm

Read and reflect on the situations below. Then look at the responses. Find out if you're a supportive friend and a positive thinker and if your friends are returning the favor.

1. You wake up one morning and it occurs to you: glow-in-the-dark paint. You'll cover your bedroom with it. It'll be like living in radioactivity! You tell your friends that night over a slice of pizza, and they laugh and laugh and laugh. For the next two weeks you endure their endless jokes. The following weekend you're painting your bedroom beige. If this were only one occurrence, you could laugh about it more, but this happens all of the time. They made fun of your Halloween costume, they made fun of the BBQ you had, they even made fun of the brand of socks you bought. What's up with your friends?

It's okay to tease your friends and to get teased every once in a while, but if your friends constantly disapprove of every little thing, it gets old real fast. If they're putting down the type of socks you buy, what are they going to think of the plans you make, the goals you set? The things that really matter to you? Find people who support your ideas and your dreams, even the crazy "living in radioactivity" ones, and be that same support system for your friends.

2. You and your roommate haven't seen each other since last school year. You start updating him about your summer. When you mention your new significant other, your roommate makes a face and tosses out a nasty remark about your boyfriend/girlfriend. Honestly, you're a bit offended. The following week, every time you mention that you're grabbing dinner with that person or going to a party with that person, your roommate has something nasty to say. What's the deal with your roommate?

Nothing stinks more than someone important in your life not being supportive of a good, healthy relationship. It's hard to hear so many disapproving comments about your significant other, especially since he or she is bringing out the best in you. If your roommate isn't going to support your relationship, share your stories with someone who will. Maybe someone who is part of another happy, healthy couple. Someone who is going to bring out the best in your relationship, not someone who is going to pick at the flaws and create problems. If you're that unsupportive roommate, you might just lose a good friend, because if your feedback is constantly negative, your friend is going to stop sharing his or her life with you. Try to focus on something positive about the relationship. Even if you don't like the person your friend is dating, you still like your friend.

3. You've been single for two years now, and it's starting to depress you. It's like everyone you know is in a relationship. You think nobody will ever find you attractive ever again. Even your dog doesn't want to sleep in bed with you tonight. He's curled up all the way on the other side of the room. You've officially shipped all the chick flicks to your recently married sister and are prepared to wander the world alone. Finally, you call your lonely friend, and talk about how neither of you are going to find anyone, so turn off the lights and bring on the Cherry Garcia. How are you doing?

Everyone has felt lonely at some point, but thinking this negatively isn't going to get you far. Open those blinds and get out in the world! Take the focus off of "finding a relationship" and put it on "finding some happiness." Make some new friends, join a new club, volunteer, spend time with your family. Lose those downer friends and find some smiling people that will bring out the smile in you. Lastly, love yourself. Let's face it, you've got some qualities about you that make you pretty great and that Cherry Garcia will never even notice.

4. You're thinking it's about time you quit smoking. Somewhere between your girlfriend being a health nut and cigarettes being seven bucks a pack, you're thinking it's a good idea. You're on the patch. You're on the gum. You're doing great. It's been a week and everyone is so proud. And then you go to a party. There's your buddy Jim, with a cigarette. "Want one?" he asks. You think it's just one … and BAM. You wake up the next morning ticked. A whole week and now you have to start over? Really? You may as well forget it.

How easy would it be to just buy another pack and call yourself a failure? If you're thinking about how your girlfriend is going to dump you if you don't quit, so you may as well just break up with her now, it's time to revamp your school of thought. Giving up on a habit is hard, and it's even harder if you don't believe in yourself. If you mess up, clean yourself up and go again. Hopefully, if you're the girlfriend in this scenario, you're the supportive kind who understands sometimes people make mistakes. Mistakes are not a reason to give up on a goal. It all goes back to *The Little Engine That Could*: "I think I can. I think I can."

5. You're having a pretty miserable day. Your professor spit on your lip in class this morning and few things are grosser than that. Nothing good was at the dining hall today and your roommate is "busy," so you volunteered to ban yourself to the residence hall lobby where everyone is watching something stupid on TV. There are no Snickers bars in the vending machine so you walk to your car, just to find your car frozen in a cube of icy snow. Today is lame! How can you think positively today?

Something you might try doing when you're having a super-lame day is thinking of the few good things that happened that day. You wore your favorite shirt and you know you looked awesome! You found two bucks in your desk drawer. If you can, laugh about the bad things that happened. *Boy, I must have looked like a tool when I had toilet paper stuck to my shoe.* It's also good to think about the good things that can come tomorrow. Maybe today was lame, but it's almost over, and hopefully after a good night sleep, tomorrow will be better. *I hear they're serving pancakes for breakfast with strawberry syrup. I have Psych tomorrow with my favorite professor. It's supposed to be sunny and warm.* If you get into the habit of focusing on the good parts of your day, you'll do it naturally all of the time.

Surrounding Yourself with Positive People: Do's and Don'ts

Do:

⊚ surround yourself with positive people;

⊚ ignore the naysayers, even when they're the people closest to you.

Don't:

⊚ allow anyone else's cynicism prevent you from reaching your dreams. Eleanor Roosevelt once said, "No one can make you feel inferior without your consent." No one can make you give up on your dreams, either, without your consent!

❝ The future belongs to those who believe in the beauty of their dreams. ❞

– Eleanor Roosevelt

8 | Think Big

I absolutely love to Think Big! After years of being afraid to tell others my big ideas for fear of sounding stupid, I've learned how fun it can be to watch someone shake her head at my latest project. So what if the world doesn't "get it"?

My 21-year-old brother, when he's feeling in the mood, makes customized wrestling action figures and occasionally sells them on eBay for extra cash. He made over $400 selling them for Christmas two years back, making over $100 on just one wrestler. Think the relatives understand that one?*

---

* *In case you're wondering, I grew up with three younger brothers. My Barbies dated Hulk Hogan, The Ultimate Warrior and Randy Macho Man Savage. Ask me sometime about my brothers' obsession with all things Hulk Hogan—I can even tell you about my favorite WrestleMania. ☺ maria@campuscalm.com.*

Charlotte Burley, a writer/producer in New York City, recently told me, "If anyone tells you that 'you can't,' use that to make you want to reach your dreams even more."

Things like GPA, letters of recommendation and awards help, but passion, persistence and a commitment to thinking big are the true driving forces behind success in life. Don't believe me? Listen to 19-year-old Brandon L. Griffin, Campus Calm's resident Youth Entrepreneurship Expert. Brandon is an entrepreneur, publisher of *Fye-Bye Magazine (For Young Entrepreneurs By Young Entrepreneurs)*, speaker, student and philanthropist. He founded his first company when he was just 10 years old and has already used his Think Big skills to help better his community in Gary, Indiana and reshape his own life.

Think Big to Go for the Billion and Make a Difference*
By: Brandon L. Griffin, Youth Entrepreneurship Expert, Campus Calm

The quiet, short and shy little boy behind the glasses—who would have thought I would be where I am today? Not me! I have been blessed tremendously, able to accomplish in just a few years what some individuals work to accomplish in a lifetime. I don't take one moment for granted.

---

* *Brandon grew up in Gary, Indiana, a city 30 miles southeast of Chicago, famous for the birth of Michael Jackson, and once infamously ranked as the "murder capital" of the United States. In an impoverished inner city, Brandon rose up to inspire youth in his community to take charge of their lives by Thinking Big. For him, financial empowerment and the entrepreneurial mindset are key.*

I am an innovator, a visionary and a results-driven leader. I always find myself thinking. Donald Trump said it best himself: "If you're going to be thinking anything, you might as well think big. It's your choice. No matter what your circumstances, nobody can stop you from thinking big."

Wise words. To me, thinking big means to plan on a grand scale, to dream up crazy scenarios and push out all thoughts of why they can't or won't work. And there's no better time than college to put those think big ideas into action. Here's how.

Build Relationships

Think about this: college is probably one of the very few times in your life that you will be able to be in direct communication with a peer group of young, relatively inexperienced individuals from so many different backgrounds. But collectively, you're the world's next generation of change makers. Be sure not to take this time lightly; instead embrace and cultivate these relationships. Grades are important, don't get me wrong, but I'm sure you've heard the phrase, "It's not what you know, it's who you know." Well, know both people and information, and you should be set for success!

Get Uncomfortable

You may be wondering, "Why in the world would I want to Think Big? I'm very comfortable staying in my dorm and working toward my degree." That's the problem—you should never be too comfortable because that means you're not taking chances. You should always be anticipating change; change allows you to push further. Yes, push further. It's often illustrated that, on average, people use only about 10 percent of their brainpower and hardly ever perform to their fullest potential.

Just think, what would life be like if we all performed to our fullest potential? Would there be no violence, illiteracy or debt? Life has been made easier in many parts of the world thanks to a few people who didn't let themselves give in to self-doubt, negative peer criticism and rejection.

Tap Your Hidden Gifts

Consider this scenario. What if you have an overlooked ability to be patient with youth? No big thing? Think again. You could help facilitate a youth program, as I did, in your local community. The local youth program could help decrease the drop-out rate of students in your community. No big thing? Think again. The program, now a proven strategy (with a special thanks to you and your ability) could easily be facilitated in another community. Now the drop-out rate among students in two communities has decreased, and you helped make it possible. Before you know it, the youth program will have a presence in hundreds of communities around the country. Chances are, if you had not thought big, you would not have become motivated to take action. Thousands of youth would now not have the luxury of pursuing a higher education, the ability to earn a higher salary and the opportunity to increase the quality of life for their families.

Pursue Your Passions

I'm sure you've heard it before: start with what you love. Sounds like a great reason to Think Big, huh? So, where do you start? It's no mystery. What are you passionate about? For me, at the age of seven, I wanted to be able to buy my own candy and toys, and selling things allowed me to earn the money to do just that. What did I sell? Whatever I was interested in at the time. I even wrote short stories, and by short, I mean one page with fat elementary school lines. I would make my brothers and sister check them out like at a library and pay a late fee for not returning them on time.

I was the youngest of four children, and the computer became my best friend when my brothers and sister were away. I learned how to create business cards, flyers, and even Websites using the computer, and then began to think about the dream to earn a living by using those same talents and interests.

Use Your Imagination

Why don't you think more people use their imagination? Maybe they're scared of what their minds dream up. I recently conducted a workshop for students between the ages of seven and ten, and you should have heard some of the ideas the kids came up with. For example, a self-refilling refrigerator and even a super remote control—BIG ideas that companies are actually working on! Somewhere down the line we stop drawing our ideas and posting them on the refrigerator for all to see. This mentality can be the determining factor in whether you just Think Big, or Think Big, go for the billion and use your ideas to really affect change in this world.

> "Somewhere down the line we stop drawing our ideas and posting them on the refrigerator for all to see."
>
> -Brandon L. Griffin

Change How You Think

When you change your way of thinking you also increase the number of opportunities you may recognize. You have to take the following and any form of the following out of your vocabulary and way of thinking: *I can't, I don't, I won't,* and *I'm not able.* You can replace them with: *I can, I do, I will,* and *I am able.* You will still encounter obstacles, particularly when neither money, nor time, nor people are at your fingertips, but in times like those you have to persevere. Learn to be patient and create solutions for problems, and soon you will be on your way.

Your Passion + Thinking Big =
Motivation & Dedication =
Results BEYOND Your Wildest
Dreams!

Persevere to Go for the Billion

Sometimes, other people won't think as big as you do. That's just reality. But don't let the naysayers stop you. They didn't stop me—I've persevered. My advice to you: don't let your age, your background, or your life history stop you from thinking big and believing in yourself. You want to be a billionaire? Who says you can't?

I started FyeBye.com when I was 15. It quickly became a successful online venture. But I wasn't finished.

When I first came up with the idea to turn FyeBye.com into a print publication, I was extremely excited! I recall calling a board meeting with my board members. All three of them were there—my mom, my older brother and my oldest brother. At that time, the board's concern was not whether I could do it, but how soon I wanted to do it. That was in mid-2004, and I wanted to launch the print magazine in the beginning of 2005. With at least some of the board's support behind me, I began my journey to turn FyeBye, the magazine, into a reality.

I was young, but I had a BIG vision for the magazine. I wanted it to be full size, full color and between 64–96 pages. Think of the advertising dollars! I began sharing that vision with individuals who I felt would offer me great insight. Instead, I felt broken after talking to almost each one. Why? Well, instead of, "Brandon, this is what you need to do in order to make that happen," I got, "Why do you want to have so many pages? That will cost too much money," or, "You should do it in black and white to make it extremely inexpensive." The most popular comment was, "Don't print it; keep it as an e-mailed newsletter." While, yes, some of these statements contained some truth, they didn't align with my vision for the publication.

So once I wiped my tears (not really), I began to think about how I could afford to turn my full-color vision into a reality. I actually used some of my mentors' suggestions. I created a self-published, black-and-white newsletter quickly and inexpensively to introduce the magazine concept to individuals. Once individuals were on the bandwagon, I used the resources I gained, whether time, money, or people (mostly money), to produce a full-color and professionally designed 16-page publication. I know it wasn't 96 pages, but it was in full color! I knew youth would not pay as much attention to a black-and-white magazine, which is why full color was so important to me.

Because I stayed true to my vision, I learned great marketing, sales, market research and other business lessons that I can utilize in the publishing industry, real estate industry or even in economic development. This is important, especially if you know me, as I'm all over the place. ☺

I was the first person under the age of 18 to be inducted into the Society of Innovators. I'm not only an innovator; I'm also an entrepreneur. Not only do I Think Big, but I also do what it takes to turn those big ideas into money-making enterprises. Because I have been blessed with this ability, I try to think, it's not "where I can't go, but where I can go," in the words of one of my mentors, Milton G. Thaxton, Jr.

Now, at the age of 19, I'm learning and experiencing—more than ever before—the importance of focusing my energy on positive things, including my goals. When we choose to focus on the positive steps we must take to reach our goals, we are making ourselves more consciously available to opportunities that will ultimately move us closer to turning that BIG idea into a BIG reality.

Putting Think Big Plans into Action

Once you have some Think Big ideas ready, you need to put them into action. Even though you haven't tried something like this before, you can do it. I'll give you some advice to help you along the way: in business, you always find yourself trying to balance three limited resources—people, money and time. It's not always easy, but it can be done.

People

Qualified and dedicated big thinkers who are committed to long-term vision are hard to find and keep. These individuals take ownership, helping achieve the set objectives and focusing more on the outcome than on personal gain.

Here's an example from my own life. I recently helped to develop a program help underserved youth recognize their potential, achieve their goals and be successful according to their own measure. I spent many, many hours "after hours" to make sure the program was a success. No amount of money could have "bought" my full attention away from my commitment to ensure the success of the youth program. It was the CEO's vision and passion that ultimately "sold" me on taking ownership, treating the program as if it were my own baby and helping make it a success. It didn't matter how much or how little monetary compensation I was going to receive. I wanted to make this program work, no matter what.

Money

Money—well, money speaks for itself doesn't it? You can never have enough, and if you have enough, you're probably spending too much! When I say, "You can never have enough," don't get me wrong, I'm not saying money is everything. It is, however, needed in most cases to make things happen. That's just how our society works.

For example, many organizations sponsor events to promote and empower youth to become entrepreneurs. While these events may be free to students, as you know, a lot of other costs are involved. The organizations need help offsetting these expenses so youth can have the luxury of experiencing a "life-changing" event at little or no cost. This is truly thinking big about what your money can do not only for you, but for others as well.

Realizing this, I have founded the Brandon L. Griffin Foundation—A Fund of Tides Foundation. I understand that money is a by-product of doing what I love to do, and that in addition to being available for material things that we all may need and want, money can also be used to help others and social causes.

Time

Finally, time: once it's gone, you can never get it back. This is another reason why thinking big is important, especially during your college years. One of my new and close mentors recently told me, "You always want to think about the end in the beginning." No, you don't want to miss out on the "college experience," but neither do you want to lose out by not taking advantage of opportunities that may open doors for you in the future. The only way you can know what doors may be opened is by taking time to think about them.

> "Strong and credible relationships are something money can't buy; it's with people and time that these are formed."
>
> -Brandon L. Griffin

For example, I will be receiving my undergraduate degree from Purdue University Calumet, which is only a few minutes away from my old high school. Because I am attending school in my hometown, I can further my education *and* continue to work in my community without the time drain of long-distance travel. That saved time is valuable. Not only do I have the luxury of living on campus and participating in student organizations, I also have the privilege of strengthening the foundation of my professional relationships within my community. Strong and credible relationships are something money can't buy; it's with people and time that these are formed.

Let's recap:

1. Don't just dream. Draw the dream, write about it and research possibilities.

2. Think Big and be positive!

3. Always persevere.

4. Remember: Time, money and people are not always in your favor. When they are, be sure to use them to your advantage to affect change in this world.

© *2008-2009 Brandon L. Griffin*

Does this mean that we have to "go for the billion" in order to be considered big thinkers? Absolutely not. Making money is important, but money is a tool that can be used for good. When making money becomes an end in itself, it becomes a hollow pursuit. As Brandon showed, thinking big and making money to generate choices for ourselves, helping others, furthering causes we believe in, holding our place in society—that's why we really "go for the billion" and remain satisfied as people.

Do you have to be a student entrepreneur in order to Think Big? Do you have to juggle academics and internships with the added pressures of trying to run a company? Again, absolutely not. The point is you can use your Think Big skills to do anything that you want in life. The sooner you realize that, the sooner you can begin to take the small Think Big steps necessary to realize your dreams. Need some tips to help you learn how to Think Big? No problem—here are 10.

10 Ways to Dare Yourself to Think Bigger

1. Be a smart observer. The next time you're at a restaurant or in a crowded subway, tune in to what people are talking about, kind of like eavesdropping but with a point! Listen to their problems and try to think of unusual ways to solve them.

2. Invest in a mentor. This one is my favorite. A mentor can inspire you to think bigger because she has been there and done that. A mentor wants to see you succeed and she's going to hold you accountable to your goals. A mentor will also help you get out of your own way to achieve success and happiness by helping you learn how to ignore your inner critic. Sometimes we sabotage our own success without even realizing we're doing it. You can find mentors everywhere. Look at your professors, community leaders and professional organizations; read writers you admire. The possibilities are endless!

3. Write down your big goals and commit to taking things one day at a time to achieve them. Enjoy the process of learning to think bigger, and don't be so concerned with the end result.

4. Start a Think Big club on campus. Poll your friends about their Think Big ideas and put them all up on a bulletin board. Motivate one another to keep thinking bigger and bigger. Don't EVER scoff at someone's Think Big idea. It could very well be the next million-dollar idea in the making.

5. Start a virtual Think Big club. Poll your friends about their Think Big ideas and post them live on a MySpace or Facebook site. Or start a Think Big blog. Bounce your big ideas around with students worldwide.

6. Remove the word *can't* from your vocabulary. Ask yourself how something can be done, instead of constantly questioning whether it can or should be done. When I launched Campus Calm, I devoted all my energies to thinking about how I could effectively use my skills to reach students around the world. If I had stopped

long enough to think about all the reasons it "couldn't" be done, you wouldn't be reading this book right now. ☺

7. Hang with some kiddos. If you're having trouble thinking big, spend an afternoon with a group of kids. Children have no problem dishing about their big, wacky, wildly impractical ideas. Listen to their stories and figure out creative ways to answer their MANY questions.

8. Believe that the world NEEDS your big ideas. Whether it's designing energy efficient automobiles, developing the latest computer software program or finding interesting ways to attract/keep young professionals in your city, our generation has a responsibility to the world to flex our creative muscles and trust in our big ideas. Isn't that inspiring?

9. Exercise your brain. For the purpose of illustration, I'm going to liken your brain to the muscles in your derriere. C'mon, go with me for a moment. Work your behind and it becomes stronger, sit on it too much and it becomes, well, flabby. The more you exercise your brain by reading, engaging in debated conversation or communicating with others you admire, the sharper your brain will become. New ideas spur more new ideas so never stop learning!

10. Relax your brain. You might be thinking, "Wait, first you're telling me I have to exercise my brain, now you're telling me to relax it?" Yep, just as you should exercise your body and relax it when it's tired, the same goes for your mind. It's all about how you relax it, though. Relaxing your mind is totally different from numbing your mind when you're stressed by reaching for a cigarette, a beer or a pint of mocha-chip ice cream.

Let's say you're stressed out. You're trying to come up with new ideas for your American Lit research paper and you're drawing a blank. Not being able to come up with new ideas is stressing you out even more. Advice: give your brain a change of scenery. When I'm blocked, I might take a walk, pop in an exercise video, listen to some music or call a friend. It doesn't hurt to procrastinate a little when you're really blocked and stressed out. When we give our minds a change of scenery it often spurs new ideas. As a writer, I know that when I'm at a loss for new things to write about, I need to get away from my computer and immerse myself in living. The same goes for you too.

Okay, I know what you're thinking. "Procrastinating on my Lit paper is what stressed me out in the first place, so I don't think procrastinating more is the answer I'm looking for." You're right. If you're trying to think up creative ideas for a paper, say, three days before it's due, you might just have to hibernate for a few days and stay away from all procrastination temptations. Cell phone, PS3, Wii, HDTV ... you get the picture.

How's your body feeling?

When you're stressed out because you procrastinated, don't waste a lot of time beating yourself up about it. Instead, take your mistake and see it as an opportunity to listen to your body and tune yourself in to how it's feeling. You probably feel like crap, huh? You're cranky, you're tired, your stomach probably hurts because of the bag of Doritos you polished off at 2:00 a.m. while attempting to edit your paper and, damn, what about tomorrow's Chem 101 assignment?

How's your skin? Is it pasty, dull, broken out? It's no accident—trust me on this. When you're stressing and sleep deprived and making poor eating decisions, your body will respond. After you turn in your paper, make

> When you're stressing and sleep deprived and making poor eating decisions, your body will respond.

an intention to try not to put your body and mind into this predicament next time. Don't ignore your body. Instead, listen to its message.

Your body is saying (screaming, actually), "SLOW DOWN. Stop procrastinating. Make wiser, healthier choices next time so you're not chained to your desk stressed beyond belief. Stop fighting my efforts to keep you healthy and start working with me. No, I'm not *Mom*—I'm simply your greatest friend in the world; we're in this together to the end so why would you want to abuse me?" Your body sure likes to chat when you actually take a second to listen to it, doesn't it? ☺

Actually, I could go on for hours, so maybe I'll just devote an entire chapter to this oh so important point. Flip the page and I promise the lessons learned will be worth it.

"Love yourself unconditionally, just as you love those closest to you despite their faults. "

– Les Brown

9 | Love Yourself

Mindset 9—love yourself—is by far the most important mindset of all. In fact, I would go so far as to argue that you can't practice any of the other mindsets to their full extent until you first learn how to love yourself. Self-assured men and women know that self-love is the key to success. No, that doesn't mean posing in front of your bedroom mirror for hours and basking in the glow of your own vanity. It does mean making your body a priority. Like taking the time to nourish it with healthy food, getting adequate sleep and exercising. Practicing relaxation. Perhaps finding the strength to quit smoking or having the resilience to never start using cigarettes, drugs or alcohol as your stress management tools in the first place.

Our society sends some harmful messages about what it means to be successful. A powerful woman recently featured in a national woman's fashion magazine said, "The secret to my success is Starbucks coffee. I think if you're willing to sacrifice some sleep, you can do anything you've always wanted, whether it's writing a book or running a marathon." When we sacrifice sleep, we sacrifice our health, and that is NOT the key to success. It is the key to stress, however. Besides, I've learned that relaxation spurs creativity far more than stress does. From one high-achiever to another, I can tell you that good health is an achievement to be VERY proud of!

Do you sacrifice sleep for success? You're not alone.
According to a Spring 2009 poll of over 2,200 college students across 40 colleges and universities, 55 percent of college students reported experiencing sleep troubles at least several days in the two week period in which they were polled, and 69 percent reported feeling tired or having little energy[*].

My Story
When I was in college, I developed poor sleep habits just like many of you. I napped a lot in the afternoon, slept poorly at night and partied until 4:00 a.m. on the weekends, crawling out of bed in time for lunch on Sunday. ☺

Because I adopted poor sleep habits in college, it was that much harder after college to set up healthy sleep habits. After a family crisis, I completely stopped sleeping regularly and experienced the worst insomnia of my life. I've watched my fair share of 3 a.m. infomercials, and no number of Ginsu Knives or Hip Hop Ab video testimonials could distract me from the anxiety of watching the clock tick away while I lay awake exhausted. At my worst, I went three days without sleeping even ten minutes. I literally felt like I was being tortured.

---

[*] *mtvU and Associated Press College Stress and Mental Health Poll, Spring 2009.*

When I couldn't sleep, I would toss and turn, cry, punch my pillow and scream, "Sleep dammit. Sleep!" Do you think that helped me fall asleep? All it did was give me a first-class ticket to a sleeping pill dependency, screwed up hormones, a sleep psychologist, a gastroenterologist for chronic stomach upset and finally, a few naturopathic practitioners and several thousand dollars in fees to help me put my life back on track.

This might sound hokey, but now every night before I go to bed, I drink a cup of herbal tea with no caffeine, turn off the lights in my living room (if I watch TV, it's something uplifting) and reflect on what I'm grateful for that day. I think about what I learned, who I met, how I felt. I choose not to focus on the mistakes I made or on my own shortcomings. When I focus on the positive, the negative starts to seem trivial and I worry less.

When I have the occasional sleepless night, I say to myself, "Okay, I can't sleep tonight. It's lousy but I'll use it as an opportunity to get some work done. It's just one night." I'll actually work through the night and make a pact with myself to take the next day off, when I'm tired anyway (it's a perk of being my own boss). I make it an intention to be really good to my body and mind that day. I might take a long walk in the park, do yoga or meditation, watch my favorite movies, read a good book for pleasure or chat with friends. I don't nap, though, even when I'm tired. Napping screws up my system, and I want to get a good night's rest the next night. When I don't "catastrophize" one sleepless night, I usually sleep fine the next night, no sleep aids necessary. Again, our bodies are giving us messages about what they need—all we have to do is be wise enough to listen.

If you need some extra help discovering for yourself what authentic self-love is, and what it means for your body and your mind, listen to the words of Amy Lademann, Campus Calm's resident Fitness Expert.

Love Yourself
By: Amy Lademann, Founder, Beyond Motion, Fitness Expert, Campus Calm

"When I loved myself enough, I learned that I needed to appreciate all that I am and all that I am not."
—Amy Lademann

Many years ago I received the book *When I Loved Myself Enough*, by Kim McMillen. This little book is made up of simple quotations all beginning with, "When I loved myself," and ending with myriad ways to find self-love. This book was my first real lesson on how to go about loving myself and living up to my full potential.

So the question remains: *What is self-love and how do you develop it?* Let me begin by asking, how do you truly feel about yourself? Do you genuinely love yourself, or are you just pretending?

How would you describe self-love? Is self-love loving the way you feel today but not tomorrow? Is self-love loving your arms but not your legs? Is self-love loving yourself when you succeed but belittling yourself when you fail? Is loving yourself about pushing your body and mind to the breaking point only to collapse from exhaustion? How do we go about learning to love ourselves fully and completely?

Step 1—Who am I, anyway?

To begin this lesson in self-love, I suggest spending 10-15 minutes responding to the following statements and questions each day ... and be HONEST. You have nothing to prove, nothing to lose and everything to gain.

1. List five things you are grateful for today.

   Idea: Perhaps it's as simple as being grateful for the sunshine or as complex as being grateful for facing your deepest fear and working to move past it.

2. Jot down one or two statements beginning with "When I loved myself enough, I ... "
   Idea: When I loved myself enough, I gave up believing life was supposed to be hard.

3. What is the one lesson you learned about yourself today?
   Idea: I learned that I spread my time too thin and attempt to accomplish too many things at one time.

4. What was your biggest stumbling block for today and how did you handle it?
   Idea: My biggest stumbling block today was finding time to exercise for more than 20 minutes, so I made the most of my time and challenged myself more than usual.

This exercise will be easier some days than others. Stick with it for at least 30 days, noticing how you feel about your life and yourself as you go through the process. Notice if you have made any changes, met any new challenges, faced any fears or just found a new group of things to be grateful for each day.

Step 2—Dream Big!

Remember the *Think Big* chapter? Thinking big is about self-love too. Ask a child what he wants to be when he grows up, and he may answer you with the same job or hobby each time. More than likely, he will throw out a different idea each time you ask. You may have stuck with that "one thing" from childhood until now, but most people change their minds repeatedly. Some people may even forget where they were heading in the first place or may feel a bit undecided.

To clear away the fog, start by dreaming about your life. Your life now while you are in school and your life once you graduate. Grab a bunch of magazines and newspapers along with some glue and poster board, or even a photo album; it's time to create some personalized art.

Making a Dream Board

Follow these steps to make a piece of art that reflects who you really are.

1. Select pictures that represent where you would like to continue your education, travel to or live.

2. Select pictures that represent the kind of feeling you want your life to have. For example, would you like to live at the beach, the mountains or in the city? Do you have a favorite hobby or sport?

3. Select items that represent your favorite color, book and music.

Take these items and create a collage that represents you. Some of these pictures may be tangible items, and other pictures may be more about a sense or feeling. This process of making a dream board is used by people all over the world to help them create the life they choose to live. Design your dream board in a way that is personal to you. If you're using a photo album, you can make notes on each page; on a poster board, make notes on the back. Jot down what you like about each picture and why it resonates with you.

This dream board or book will keep you focused and on track. No matter who you are, where you are from, how good your grades are and whether or not you play a sport, you can design your life and accomplish your dreams if you know how to begin and in which direction to head.

Step 3—Take care of you, your body, your temple

Now that you are getting to know more about yourself, it's time to check your daily routine to make sure everything you do supports your body and your mind. Answer the following questions honestly.

1. Do you sleep between seven and eight hours a night?

2. Do you drink at least eight glasses of water each day to remain hydrated and to flush the toxins out of your body?

3. Do you eat three meals and two small snacks each day to balance your blood sugar so that your brain and body work synergistically? Each meal and snack should contain as many fresh fruits, veggies and lean proteins as possible. Try to limit processed foods, things with sugar and artificial sugars, along with fried foods. You should eat foods that will keep you healthy and feeling your best. Loving yourself means taking care of *you* the best way possible.

4. Are you active for at least 30 minutes each day? Anything from a quick walk or jog to swimming, playing a sport, dancing or Roller-

blading counts. Any sport or activity you enjoy doing that makes your heart pound and your body sweat is a good thing. Most people who develop an active and healthy lifestyle while they're in school continue an active and healthy lifestyle throughout their lives.

5. Do you smoke? If you do—QUIT! There is nothing healthy, positive or self-loving about smoking. Your health is a complete product of the actions you take. If you take care of your body, it will take care of you.

Step 4—Be kind to yourself

What do you consider to be fun? Do you take time every day to cultivate your sense of spirit and creativity?

Feeling confident and cultivating your inner awareness are keys to achieving self-love and appreciation. We all know people who exude positive energy and a zest for life. It comes from within. In order to tap into your inner sparkle, you must take time each day to cultivate and explore who you really are and what you're made of. It's easy to get caught up in watching TV, studying or staying out too late. But to truly feel healthy, balanced and restored, you need to take care of YOU.

The best act of self-love is to cut yourself some slack. Give yourself the same chances you would offer your best friend. When you make mistakes, remember, at least you tried. When the end result isn't exactly what you had anticipated, know that there is always another time to try harder, work smarter and affect the result. Know that from every action there is a valuable lesson to be learned; then use that lesson to your advantage the next time.

> "The best act of self-love is to cut yourself some slack."
>
> -Amy Lademann

No one is perfect, and everyone is unique. Each day you have numerous opportunities to live your best life possible and create balance between your body, mind and soul. Make choices each day that support who you are and what you want out of your life. Know that the decisions you make today may impact your future, so taking the time to explore your true self will truly teach you how to love yourself.

© *2008-2009 Amy Lademann*

Campus Calm had the opportunity to speak with Natalie Butler, our resident Nutrition Expert, about how a healthy lifestyle starts with self-love, no dieting necessary. Natalie recently completed her dietetic internship through Marywood University and is currently a registered dietitian. She's also the founder of NutritionByNatalie.com, a nutrition consulting firm devoted to improving the health and wellness of individuals, families and businesses.

Q&A with Natalie Butler on Self-Love, Nutrition and Health

Maria: How has learning to love yourself helped you find success and happiness in business and in life?

Natalie: Learning to love myself evolved by my discovering how I could use my talents, interests and skills to benefit others. It's very easy to be selfish in this world, think only of yourself and little of others, prove you're better than everyone else, have the bigger house, drive the nicer car

… but life is so much deeper than that. I found that as my interest in food developed into a passion for nutrition and health, I could use that to benefit everyone around me. When I am concerned with what I can give to this world, not what I can receive, I am in such a content place. So my self-love didn't actually evolve by my focusing on myself, it evolved as I focused on others, and that's actually how my business came into being. I found that the best way to help people the way I wanted to was to start my own business. There is nothing more fulfilling and nothing that can make you love yourself more than helping change a life forever.

◎ ◎

> "When I am concerned with what I can give to this world, not what I can receive, I am in such a content place."
>
> -Natalie Butler

◎ ◎ ◎

M: What does being healthy personally mean to you?

N: Being healthy means, to me, living life to the fullest. We all have so much potential, so much we can accomplish, so much we can contribute, but if we lose our health those opportunities are cut short. One of my favorite quotes is, "You can have all the riches in the world, but if your health fails you, you have nothing." And health is an all-encompassing term. It doesn't just mean eating healthy foods; it involves every aspect of health: reducing stress, eating vegetables, limiting sweets and processed foods, consuming healthy fats, being active daily, cutting out chemicals, getting adequate rest, not relying on medications when the underlying cause hasn't been addressed, drinking enough water, stretching, living in a supportive community or family and most importantly, taking personal responsibility for your own health and your own life.

So health, for me, is a choice I make every day. Sometimes it comes easily, sometimes it doesn't, but it's my choice, and only I can truly choose to be healthy or not. The responsibility doesn't lie with others. In our society, taking a pill has become the easy "way to regain your health." But popping a pill will never replace or equal making healthy lifestyle choices.

M: Can you offer motivation to students as to why self-love is such an important part of nutrition and overall wellness?

N: In simple terms, making your health a priority is the ultimate display of love and affection for yourself. If you love someone else, you will perhaps spend time cooking for them, giving them gifts, caring for them. It shouldn't be any different for ourselves. Whatever you make time for in your life, you have made it a priority, which it means it is important to you. For example, if you're a student, you've made your education a priority. You will spend years studying, learning, reading, listening, doing projects and taking tests. Through your education, you're investing in your future and your life. And health is the same way. You must value yourself enough to take time to invest in your health. The ultimate show of your love for yourself is that you will spend time doing your best to ensure that your body will be healthy, your quality of life will be optimal and that you can live life to the fullest.

M: Why don't diets work, and why should eating healthy and resting your body be about wellness and not just appearance?

N: To put it bluntly, diets are quick fixes. And most of the time, they're unhealthy, extreme and unbalanced. Many people view diets as a way to reach a goal, but rarely do fad diets translate into lifelong healthy lifestyle changes. Humans are emotional and psychological creatures, and many times, the emotional and behavioral patterns behind the reasons someone eats the way he does are not addressed, so eventually the person resorts back to his old habits.

In addition, many people go on diets to look a certain way on the outside, to slim down, to drop weight fast, to appear "healthy." But health is not all appearance. Young people have the advantage of quicker metabolisms, and if they view health only as appearance, they may eat whatever they want as long as they remain thin. If we could turn people inside out and view the insides of many "healthy appearing" people, I think we would be shocked at the true states of their bodies. Even athletes, who exercise so much they can typically eat whatever they want and maintain a thin physique, don't automatically qualify as healthy. Being healthy doesn't necessarily equal being thin.

M: Do you think that a healthy body starts with a healthy mind?

N: Definitely. Because your perception of life and the way you think will dictate how you live. If you view exercise as a negative thing, something you dread, something you're being made to do, you're much more apt to give up, look for an excuse to not go, quit and just be miserable. Or if you view eating healthy negatively, because you're missing out on eating desserts all the time or you can't have your favorite chips every day that's the kind of thinking that will sabotage your health goals.

Instead, be positive, think positively and be around people who are positive and supportive. Remind yourself of the benefits of any change you make: you will have more energy, you will sleep better, you will feel better, you won't have as many headaches and you won't get sick as much. It's this way of thinking, this healthy mindset, that will help you stay motivated to keep moving toward your goals and help you stay committed to a healthy lifestyle.

I'm thrilled that Natalie brought up the point that appearance doesn't necessarily equal health. Young people, especially young women, face so many pressures to conform to a too-thin perfect ideal that's often unhealthy to maintain. In March 2008, I interviewed college women about body image and the pressures to look perfect for spring break. I asked them what they thought makes a person beautiful. One young woman responded, "Being comfortable in your own skin is the highest form of beauty you can reach, and not caring what other people think. I wish I could be more like that, and I try to be more like that, but it's hard."*

I recently received an e-mail from a mom who asked: *How can we get more young women to stop hating their bodies?*

First of all, body image is *not* just a female problem. When I walk into my local health food store, I often see a group of guys asking about the protein powder and weight gainer. A friend of mine who's a personal trainer says that he sees just as many guys over-exercising

---

* *"Young Women Speak Out about Body Image on College Campuses"*: www.campuscalm.com/collegewomen_bodyimage.html. *Check out "March and April Madness Beach Bod Style" to see how college men responded:* www.campuscalm.com/march_madness.html.

at the gym as girls. Men want to bulk up and women want to slim down. We're all trying to live up to unrealistic standards of beauty. Women are simply encouraged to talk about their feelings, while men are encouraged to act macho and pretend there's no problem.

We have to get ALL students to view eating whole, nutritious foods and exercising as a way to respect their bodies and to promote an active, healthy lifestyle. The emphasis shouldn't be just on looking good in your jeans. America's obsessive quest to look good as opposed to feel good is why we so easily fall prey to the $30 billion per year diet industry and the $26 billion cosmetic surgery industry. When you're treating your body with all the love and respect it deserves, you will, in turn, look better. Campus Calm wants students to view good health as an end in itself, though, and not just as a means to look better. One thing I've learned post-graduation is that when I'm taking care of my body, I sleep better, I'm more creative, alert and productive … and I look better too, which is just a fun fringe benefit.

Understand that how we see ourselves in the mirror determines how we see ourselves in every aspect of our lives. If we spend 20 minutes in front of a mirror criticizing every inch of our bodies, how can we possibly act confidently once we leave our bedrooms? You can primp, sculpt and make over your body many times throughout your life, but the image you have of yourself lasts a lifetime. So make it a good one.

If you want to download and print a larger copy of the "Loving Yourself" exercise, visit:
www.campuscalm.com/book/exercises

Need some extra help with the whole concept of self-love? Check out the following reflective exercise.

Loving Yourself—A Reflective Exercise
By: Kristen Szustakowski, Editorial Intern, Campus Calm

Basics:

My name: _____

Age: _____

Favorite color: _____

Favorite food: _____

Favorite movie: _____

Family:

One characteristic I got from my mother: _____
_____

One characteristic I got from my father: _____
_____

One thing about my family I would never change: _____
_____

Friends:

Name one friend:_____

_____

Why I appreciate this friend: _____

_____

_____

One thing I have done for this friend that made him/her smile: ____

_____

_____

One thing this friend has done for me that has made me smile: ____

_____

_____

Appearance:

Three things I love about my body: _____

_____

_____

Three things I am grateful that my body can do for me: _____

_____

_____

One thing I will do to make myself healthier: _____

_____

_____

One outfit I look great in (Yes, guys have outfits too even if they won't admit it...): _____

_____

One outfit I feel great in: _____

_____

_____

Soul:

Three things I'm good at: _____

_____

_____

Two things I'm not good at: _____

_____

_____

One activity that makes me feel "me": _____

_____

_____

One TV/movie character I can identify with: _____

_____

_____

Why? _____

_____

_____

One thing that makes me incredibly happy: _____

_____

_____

One thing that makes me sad: _____

_____

_____

One thing that makes me angry: _____

_____

_____

One thing I'm afraid of: _____

_____

_____

One important lesson I learned this year: _____

_____

_____

One way I'm smarter than I was last year: _____

_____

_____

Three things I can't live without: _____

_____

_____

Three things I could live without: _____

_____

_____

Heroes:

Three people I admire: _____

_____

_____

The strengths they have: _____

_____

_____

The weaknesses they have: _____

_____

_____

Dreams:

One goal I have this week: _____

_____

_____

One goal I have this year: _____

_____

_____

Three things I'd like to do in my lifetime: _____

_____

_____

One thing I'd like to get better at: _____

_____

_____

One thing I've always wanted to do/say but haven't yet: _____

_____

_____

What am I waiting for? _____

_____

_____

One thing I would change about the world: _____

_____

_____

One step I could take in that direction: _____

_____

_____

This exercise was designed to help you think about yourself. Remember the *Focus Inward* chapter? You can't find authentic success and happiness until you look inside for answers. I argue that you cannot truly love and appreciate yourself until you look inside as well. Hopefully, this exercise helped you to realize that your unique mix of characteristics make you a wonderfully beautiful person. That's why you should love who you are, from your talents to your flaws.

Look over your answers. What do you see? Did you answer them truthfully, and if you didn't, why? Is there a positive or negative tone to your answers?

Reflect on how you felt answering these questions. Were they easy to answer or did you have a hard time with them? Did they make you feel good about yourself? Did you realize things about yourself you hadn't realized until now?

Get used to thinking about yourself in a positive way, especially when it comes to your flaws. We all can't be perfect at everything we do! It's good to not be good at some things, as long as we can maintain a healthy attitude.

Lastly, don't let this be the only time you answer these questions. Think about these questions a month from now. A year from now. Reflect on how you have changed, and don't be afraid to add your own self-reflection questions to the list. Be brave enough to dig into your own ingredients. Discover yourself. Love yourself.

Love Yourself Lowdown

Do:

◎ commit to respecting your body for all the ways it serves you. Can you walk to class? Dance at a party? Throw a football? Ski down a slope? That's plenty to thank your body for;

◎ nourish your body with healthy, whole foods, which will give you more energy, strength and endurance to live life to the fullest. Remember that eating healthy is not just about looking good in your jeans, but about how it makes you feel inside and out;

◎ start a campus-wide blog or Facebook group where students post their ideas on how to make it "cool" to be healthy. Give students a voice in the process. Share your own "Stress Less" tips, start challenging one another to get enough sleep and listen to your bodies. Now that is something a really special student leader would do; ☺

◎ go easy on yourself and laugh at your mistakes. After all, you're fabulously human and are allowed MANY moments of imperfection.

Don't:

◎ diet. Ever;

◎ berate yourself for your flaws. Whether it's a pimple, a few extra pounds or one less-than-stellar test grade … relax! Celebrate your strengths and remember that our flaws make us human and—therefore—relatable to others. Can you imagine how boring life would be if we all were perfect at everything? ☺

" **Getting there isn't half the fun—it's all the fun.** **"**

– Robert Townsend

10 | Have Fun

I bet that you will almost never hear the message in this chapter's title—that one of the keys to a successful life is having more fun—but it's absolutely true. **Life is supposed to be fun!** Even busy college students are supposed to have fun. When I was sitting where you are as a college student, I didn't see that. I spent four years of my life working, working, working, and whenever I stopped working, I felt guilty about my pile of homework that never seemed to stop growing.

You know how much it irritates you when middle-agers tell you that your college years are supposed to be the best years of your life? Between mounds of homework, that crappy retail job, work study, and trying to figure out what you want to do with the rest of your life … fun? Yeah, right!

While high school and college aren't all fun and games, they shouldn't be the worst years of your life either. There has to be a healthy balance between studying your student years away and spending your academic career in a drunken stupor.

After complaining to a former professor about my lack of time to enjoy my college years, he advised, "Maria, take 30 minutes each day and have fun, do something for yourself. It helps." So that's what I'm going to leave you with today: make time each day for fun. If you're thinking, "I don't have time for fun, I barely have time for sleep," I'm going to tell you something I wish someone had told me: prioritize your schedule better, and if you don't have time for you every day, find something to cut back on. Maybe it's an extracurricular activity, maybe it's an hour at your part-time job, maybe it's something that you feel like you "should" be doing but you really don't find that much enjoyment in.

Take those few precious moments that you steal for yourself and take a hike in the woods, ride your bike, sit under a tree and think or go for ice cream with friends. If you can learn how to balance work and fun and prioritize your time in a self-focused way *before* you leave your school years behind, I guarantee you'll lay the foundation to realize that happy life you're working so hard to achieve.

And that, dear friends, is what true success is all about.

Create an Intentional Legacy
By: Beverly Coggins, Time Management Expert,
Campus Calm

I love my life!! As a professional organizer and the foster parent of teenage girls, I get to use my gifts and talents on a daily basis. One of those gifts is time management, which I draw upon in order to pull off both of these areas at the same time.

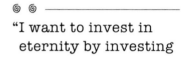

I want to leave a legacy that will out-last me—I want to invest in eternity by investing in people—my own grown children, my foster children, friends, family, clients and even strangers! My passions are to help people make home

"I want to invest in eternity by investing in people."
-Beverly Coggins

a refuge and to help people live in peace rather than chaos. My legacy, passions and gifts give me context, which guides me in determining how I spend my time. This context makes it easier to say no to activities that don't fit with the direction I'm going.

I learned my time management skills while in college and balancing a full load, working 20 hours a week and enjoying an active social life. I needed to work, I wanted to finish school in four years and I didn't want to give up my social life or my sleep to do so. So I learned to squeeze the most out of every minute—always carrying with me something to study or read when I had a few extra minutes or when a class or activity was cancelled. I eliminated activities that didn't contribute to my goals, but I still had lots of fun doing the things I wanted to do.

It was during my college years that I started identifying the legacy I wanted to leave, my passions, my gifts and my priorities. I created goals for each semester and planned my semester accordingly, trying to create a balance between work, school, my own personal development and fun.

I'm so thankful I learned these things while in college. I continue to sit down once or twice a year to re-examine my life—passions and priorities, even legacies, can change during different stages of life. Even though my legacy of wanting to invest in people has not changed, how that has materialized over the years has looked different at various times.

Having a grasp of what matters to me has helped me to determine what jobs to consider, where I volunteer my time and how I spend my discretionary time.

I started out working with college students, helping them determine their legacies, passions, priorities and gifts. Over time and as my life changed, I switched my focus to helping women do the same thing.

I became fascinated with personality profiles and pursued training in that area. As a result, I started my own business helping people master the key areas of life and business: interpersonal relationships, organizing one's time and space and determining one's focus and priorities. I added team-building seminars, training seminars and personal coaching to my tool belt.

As time went on, I took my organizing skills to a new level, and the majority of my business comes from professional organizing at present. I have discovered that as I keep growing and learning, doors open to new avenues. I have enjoyed the process, the journey on which life has taken me.

I recently turned some of my discretionary time into a series of books called *1-2-3 ...Get Organized*, books and workbooks that help people organize their time and space one area at a time.

My passions, the legacy I want to leave and the desire to obtain some passive income motivated me to pursue this project. It was challenging to find time to write the books, but by using time I could have easily wasted, I was able to carve out moments when I could write. I didn't sacrifice a balanced life, though—I'm still committed to having fun, getting enough sleep and growing as a person.

It took a couple of years. The books started out as e-books. Next, I sent them to a graphic designer to turn them into cute, colorful, glossy books. The final step was the publisher. While the books were being printed, I worked on the workbooks. It all came together when all 15 of the books and workbooks were launched at the same time. Even though all this sounds like a lot of work, it was fun for me. I was learning new things, which was invigorating! In the midst of it all, I made sure I took time to play, be with my family and do activities that refreshed me.

I don't think this series would have been published had I not been intentional about the legacy I wanted to leave, the passions and priorities I wanted to pursue and the gifts I wanted to use. When you take time to identify these and live your life accordingly, you too will love your life!

—— ◎ ◎ ◎ ——

Quiz: Is Your Fun Factor Just Right?

By: Kristen Szustakowski, Editorial Intern, Campus Calm

Once upon a time, you went for a walk around your college campus and realized there were three types of fun. They were all sitting there, right before your eyes! Small fun, big fun, and fun that is just right.

Read and answer the questions below to find out what sized fun you're sitting in.

1. The weekend is finally here! What are your plans?

   a. Bogie is getting a keg! Now I just have to write to all the professors I have Monday and tell them I'm coming down with something: a severe case of alcohol tolerance and Guitar Hero skill!

   b. Plans? You're funny. I have projects to do. I have to study for mid-terms. I have a paper that's going to take the rest of my life. Don't expect to see me until graduation.

   c. I'm going to get all of my work done during the day Saturday so I can stop by this Bogie character's party Saturday night for a few hours and still have free time on Sunday before study group to play Halo and grab coffee with Mom.

2. It's Monday morning. What are you up to?

   a. Writing the conclusion to the paper due ten minutes ago ... now why isn't the printer working?!

   b. I've got a few minutes before class. I'm going to jog around the hallways so I can cram my exercise into my busy schedule. Excuse me, pardon me, coming through... .

   c. I'm going to sip my Starbucks and talk to the girl who sits in front of me. There's a test today but I'm feeling pretty confident so I'm going to relax a few moments before I bust out the #2s and ace this thing!

3. Which list looks most like this week's To Do list?

   a. Garage Band tournament, hang with my new girlfriend, poker tournament, hang with my new girlfriend, make roommate write my paper, SparkNotes that book for English, buy a bigger TV, hang with my new girlfriend.

   b Well, there's that oceanography extra credit and that history project. I ran out of Post-its so I hired a secretary to pick up a new pack as well as do my laundry because with this test in Shakespeare coming up, I don't have time for silly tasks.

   c History project, movies with Matt, English paper, study group, Hall Council meeting, coffee with Shelly, research at the library, drinks with my BFF! Extra credit if I've got the time and if I'm in the mood.

4. When was the last time you colored a picture? Went for a walk around the block? Watched a sunset? Played a videogame? Played Apples to Apples? Read a book because you wanted to? Painted? Wrote a poem that wasn't for a class? Had a snowball fight? Tie-dyed? Picked up seashells? Lay in the grass and felt the sun on your face? Played hopscotch? Hula-hooped? Planned a practical joke on your friend? Made jewelry? Sat under a tree and people-watched? Made a paper airplane? Raced a friend to the corner and back? Played with clay? Skipped rocks over a pond? Any of these things?

   a. Yeah. Today. Drunk.

   b I don't think I did most of that when I was five years old. Why would I waste my time doing that now when I have important things I really need to get done?

   c Of course I do those things! Not as much as I'd like to, but when I have free time, I love coloring and playing games and having fun!

5. How often do you have fun?

   a. I'm always having fun. It's college. College is meant for fun.

   b. I don't have time for fun. Once I get my degree there will be time for fun.

   c. I try to whenever I can. Some days there's just too much work but the days when I have the time, you bet I'm using it for myself!

Check Your Scorecard

Mostly A's: This fun is toooo big!
<u>Get stuff done, then have fun.</u> You absolutely should have fun in college, but remember the first reason you're there: an education. That needs to be your first priority. The parties can come later. If you take the time to get the important stuff done before the fun, you will not only succeed in school and fun, but you will also feel better about having fun, because you won't have anything hanging over your head. You can really be in the moment.

Mostly B's: This fun is toooo small!
<u>Cool it. Live a bit!</u> Where's your fun? It's almost non-existent! It doesn't matter what your major is. No major is so hard that you can't take a few minutes every once in a while to do something for yourself just because you deserve it. And if you think you're going to work all through college and have your fun when you graduate, think again. If you've created a work-only life in college, your life after college isn't going to be any different unless you do something about it! So cool it. Live a bit!

Mostly C's: This fun is just right!
<u>Work and fun together makes college better!</u> You've got a fantastic mix of work and play. You know when it's time to get focused and when it's time to relax. When you mix work and fun together, you're making college better because you know why you're there. To get an education and to have fun—and you're pretty awesome at both! Keep it up, Goldilocks!

As you might imagine from reading this book, my fun factor in college was definitely too small. I crammed in so much work that by the time I graduated I really was ready for retirement ... with no 401k or health insurance plan.

Kristen is absolutely right—if you say to yourself, "I'll make college all about work, then play after graduation," you won't just stop working as soon as the diploma is in your hands. You have to make that conscious choice to slow down a bit. Graduating with anxiety-induced health problems forced me to slow down and reevaluate my life. To allow time for joy and fun. To star in my own reality show called, *Maria, Meet the Present.* I often say that I experienced a twentysomething crisis to save me from an even bigger midlife crisis.

If you want to save yourself a twentysomething crisis and a midlife crisis, consider practicing the following.

Do:

◉ make time for fun every day, even if it's just 30 minutes;

◉ prioritize your schedule before someone else prioritizes it for you. Remember when you were a kid on summer vacation and whined, "Mom, I'm sooo bored." How did she respond? "I'll find you something to do!" It usually involved a broom or a dishcloth, correct? And you could have been playing kickball with the neighbors' kids if you just would have gone outside and prioritized fun. ☺

Don't:

◉ ever let anyone tell you that less fun = more success. They're wrong and they're going to burn out, if they haven't already.

Here's the greatest lesson that I learned post-graduation:

Success isn't feeling like you have to do everything and be everything to all people. Happiness IS Success. ☺

———— ◎ ◎ ◎ ————

✔ Checklist: Foolish Fun in 30 Minutes or Less
By: Maria Pascucci and Kristen Szustakowski

If you're the type of student who's been working nonstop since you crawled down the birth canal, do you even know how to have foolish fun without hurting your academic experience? Don't worry, my intern Kristen and I are here to help you! Give some of the following ideas a try. Post your experiences and Have Fun ideas on the Campus Calm forum here: www.campuscalm.com/forum.

Kristen: Go on a scavenger hunt! Get your shopping done and have fun at the same time by exchanging grocery lists with a friend. You then have thirty minutes to gather all the items and meet in front of the check out. Ready ... set ... GO!

Maria: Have five minutes to spare? Do the Electric Slide in your dorm room. C'mon you know that every time someone says the words, "It's electric," you want to get your boogie on.

☐ **K:** Grab your favorite CD and a couple of your friends. Get in the car and drive. Sing the music as loud as you can. Feel free to dance. If you're really feeling gutsy, keep the windows rolled down and watch for weird looks by passengers driving by. But don't forget to keep your eyes on the road. ☺

☐ **M:** Hit the local bowling alley for a quick game with your best bud. If you can carve out some extra time, play two or three. Hint: Sunday night discounts are sweet. Saturday night, you'll pay to play. And don't worry about scoring a perfect 300. If you stink, play bumper bowling. It's just as fun.

☐ **K:** Bust out the old roller skates you haven't seen since ninth grade and go for a spin around campus. If you go with friends, try to find things in the area none of you have ever seen before.

☐ **M:** Play Twister ... sober. You'll probably be able to hold your right hand on red and your left foot on green a lot longer sans the margaritas. Bonus: Twister will prepare your body to handle a mean downward-facing dog yoga pose.

☐ **K:** You're never too old to play hide-and-seek, or tag, or capture the flag. Get some friends together and relive your childhood. See how many other students on campus you can get to join you.

☐ **M:** Watch "World Record Twister Game" on You Tube. It's pretty intense.

☐ **K:** Take the seasons by storm! Is it snowing? Make a fort, a snow angel, a giant snowman. If it's sunny, play with chalk and pick flowers. Rake fall leaves into a pile and jump in. Stomp in rain puddles. Take a walk in the sun. Fly a kite. Enjoy thirty minutes of whatever nature is giving you.

☐ **M:** Carve out a weekly 30-minute fun date with your friends. Post this sign to your door when playtime's in session: "Students at Recess: <u>No</u> School Talk Allowed." If you're really cheesy you can even decorate your sign with yellow glitter and smiley stickers.

☐ **K:** Board Games! Sorry, Life, Trouble? All of these can be purchased somewhat cheaply (or "borrowed" from Mom and Dad's basement) and are a quick way to have fun with friends. And if you've got longer than 30 minutes, there's always Monopoly.

☐ **M:** Or Pictionary. Yes, you CAN win while scribbling stick figures. If I have to draw an animal and you're on my team, just start screaming, "Dog, pig, cat, gorilla, giraffe, lama" because every animal I draw looks the same.

☐ **K:** Take on a long-term project you can work on for 30 minutes every day. A scarf you're knitting. A scrapbook. A photo album for a friend.

☐ **M:** Play dress up. Who says you have to wait until Halloween to break out the Batman costume? Feelin' like wearing those Dorothy Gale inspired red sparkle heels to class? When class gets boring, maybe you can click your feet and get whisked away to casa de numero uno. There's no place like home, you know?

Campuscalm

10 Affirmations to Calm College Student Stress

1. I will allow myself enough sleep each night to fully rest my body, recharge my batteries and support my immune system to protect against illness.

2. I will exercise my body in ways that I enjoy, even if that means squeezing in a 20-minute walk between classes.

3. I will pay attention to my emotions and find positive ways to calm my mind & body down when I'm stressed. I will try deep breathing, yoga or I'll call a friend up and do something fun!

4. I will follow my intuition about what's right for my future and not be swayed by the expectations and demands of others.

5. Before I say "yes" (again) to something or someone, I will ask myself, "Is this new task in alignment with my goals? Will saying 'yes' make me happy? What will I have to sacrifice if I say 'yes' to this new activity?" Be honest and don't be afraid to put your own needs first every now and then!

6. I will be grateful for the body I was born with, taking time to appreciate its unique wonder. I will stand proud knowing that I am able to judge my own body by my standards, not by unrealistic media/advertiser standards.

7. Sometimes, I will leap before I look, take chances and give my dreams the chance to come true.

8. I will stop worrying about the future and start living right in the present. Really, really LIVING. Day by day, taking a moment to appreciate things just the way they are. I will make college about learning and relationship building instead of stressing over every individual grade—a flawless résumé means nothing if I'm burned out and unhappy before my career even begins!

9. I will nourish my body with healthy, whole foods, which will give me more energy, strength and endurance to live life to the fullest. I will remember that eating healthy is not about looking good in my jeans, but about how it makes me feel inside and out.

10. I will remember to go easy on myself and to embrace my mistakes as learning opportunities. After all, I'm fabulously human and am allowed MANY moments of imperfection.

Laugh a little more. Worry a little less. This could be your healthiest year yet!

Want to hang this list up in your bedroom/dorm? Visit **www.campuscalm.com/book/exercises** to download and print your poster.

Appendix A
Q&A with David Mammano

Campus Calm's College-Planning Expert and publisher of *Next Step Magazine*

Now that you've learned about each of my 10 mindsets to *authentic* success and happiness, it's time to put it all together in a succinct way. David Mammano, one of my *favorite* mentors, fellow western New Yorker and Campus Calm expert, offered his first person experience of how each mindset helped him to build a happy, successful and purposeful life.

Maria: How does a lifelong love of learning contribute to a happy and successful life? Please share your personal experiences on this subject.

Dave: The moment you stop learning, your brain shrivels up and dies. Just as you need to put good food into your body to help it perform at the highest level, you need to put good, new and updated information into your brain for it to function. What I do to continue my knowledge—I had enough of college after four years because I'm not very good at sitting still in a classroom— is read every morning. I get up at 5 a.m. and I read for an hour. I read a good book, usually business related. Then I get on the treadmill or the elliptical for another hour and listen to an audio book on my iPod—so I continue learning. I'm much better with audio because it's a better sensory experience for me.

I've also joined Entrepreneurs Organization (EO), a world-wide network of business owners. (Everyone should join a professional organization.) EO is a peer-to-peer learning group—we're all growing our businesses, learning things and making mistakes, and going through obstacles. Being an entrepreneur can be lonely at times because your friends—and a lot of times your employees—don't know or maybe don't care what you're going through. It looks like a glamorous life, and sometimes it is, but sometimes it's very stressful.

EO offers an intensive learning program, spread out over three years, called the MIT Entrepreneurial Masters Program. Sixty participants from around the world meet for five days each year and are exposed to world-class thinkers and business leaders.

To challenge myself, I also meet with people who I believe are 10 rungs above me on the ladder. I recently attended a conference where the keynote speaker was the CEO of Forbes.com. I sat in the front row during his speech, and afterward I was the first one to go up and talk to him. I got his business card, and I'm setting up a meeting with him. I want to learn from these people who have been there and done it. That really fuels my fire as an entrepreneur. Think of people that you would be like, "Wow, I would love to sit down with that person." Then try it. Sometimes you can't make it happen, but sometimes you can. That's how you build up your network.

M: When I was super stressed in college, a professor once advised that I "take a half hour each day and live deliberately." Do you live deliberately each day? How?

D: I think you should live deliberately all the time, not just a half hour a day. The average American works 84,000 hours in his lifetime—I think those should be deliberate hours. You don't want to finish that last hour and say, "Man that sucked!" That's why I chose to be an entrepreneur: I do want to be deliberate in everything I do. We all have to suck it up occasionally and do something we don't want, but I think we should strive to constantly live the way we want to live. Reading and working out in the morning puts me in a great place for the rest of the day. I exercise my brain and my body. That allows me to start the day with a really great grip. If you don't have that great grip going in, maybe that tornado may take you where you don't want to be. The happiest people *live* rather than just *exist*. They have a purpose and there's a strategy to their lives.

"The happiest people live rather than just exist. They have a purpose and there's a strategy to their lives."

-Dave Mammano

M: Campus Calm believes that the time you set aside on a regular basis for fun and relaxation actually helps to make for a successful and happy life. Could you share some personal stories about how learning to balance fun with work has led you to enjoying a happy and successful life?

D: You see a lot of people who are successful in business but whose families suffer. It's very important for me to strive for success in both. I really try to be home by 5:30 p.m. every day. I have dinner with my family every night unless I'm traveling. I think it's very important to have that balance. If you're out of balance, it will affect you physically after a while and emotionally too. Once again, aiming for balance is a very purposeful strategy.

Many times, my family will go to sleep around 9 p.m. and I'll get back up and work. I don't want to do it when they're up. My son is 3½ and my daughter is two. I want to play with them. I'm at peace with myself. I feel great. I like my life. It's a simple life at the end of the day. I don't get caught up in excesses and materialism and all that stuff, either. I'd rather have a nice home-cooked meal with my family than go out to a fancy restaurant.

M: How has your ability to Think Big contributed to your success? How would you recommend students craft the element of thinking big? How can they learn to trust their big ideas?

D: Thinking big has been totally responsible for my success. You have to think of something that is perceived as totally unattainable to most people. You have to see that you want to give it a shot. If you just want to be like the average person, then you'll think small. The universe is a pretty wild thing in that it usually gives you what you ask of it. If you're going to ask a lot and you work hard, the universe will give you a lot. It's like a bank in that the more deposits you put into it, the more you'll get out in the future in choices. You have to think of things that are just crazy, insane. What do you have to lose?

Here's a crazy idea. *Next Step* needs new office space, so I went to a local college. I said, "Hey, you have a journalism school. How about you give me free office space and I'll let your journalism students work at the magazine?" Imagine you were trying to recruit high school students to your college. You could tell future journalism students that you have a national magazine at your college. Think what a great selling tool that is! The college loved the idea, but it became too sticky trying to put a for-profit business on a not-for-profit campus. I think you have to push the envelope; otherwise you're not going to get any place. I love the saying, *A boat safe in the harbor rots.*

So, how do students learn to Think Big? First, they need to craft the element of just thinking. When do people find the time to think today? Teens are IMing, they're on their cell phones and they have their podcasts. When do they have the time to just think? Part of thinking big is innate—some people do it naturally. But you can also train yourself to Think Big. You take a small risk, and it works out, and you build some confidence. The most important thing is to take that first step and try something a little crazy.

When I started *Next Step Magazine* I said, "What's the worst that could happen?" I wasn't married, didn't have kids and my parents lived close by, so if I couldn't pay my rent I could move home for a little while. If I left my job for the magazine, but it didn't work out, I could always go get my job back or find another one. So think of the worst-case scenario. If it's not that bad, what do you have to lose? It's easier to do it when you're younger because you have less to lose.

Take baby steps and realize that you fail only when you stop trying. If *Next Step* had failed, I would have started another business and learned from my past mistakes. The trick is to not make those same mistakes again.

M: Campus Calm believes that self-love is a huge element of success in life. How do you learn to silence your inner critic and hold yourself in the highest regard?

D: I think you have to be consistent with who you are as a person and be consistent with your actions. You start to not like yourself when you do things that you know deep inside are not consistent with who you are and what your values are. When you really start to be consistent with your vision of what's right, you just start to like yourself more. Those self-doubting voices start to disappear because you're being consistent with your character and your values. I think you see a lot of people depressed or just not happy with themselves because they're just not walking the walk 24/7. It's hard to do—especially in America where there is a lot of temptation and shortcuts. If you have an inner voice that's telling you you're not good enough, if you're consistent with yourself, you'll have the power to say, "Well, that's a bunch of crap. I know I'm good enough—I just did it." That builds your self-esteem, step by step.

M: Campus Calm believes that when we sacrifice sleep, we sacrifice our health and that's the key to stress, *not* success. Could you share a personal story of how relaxation spurred your creativity in a way that stress never could?

D: If I don't get seven hours of sleep a night, I'm not good to anybody. It's all about balance. What determines a successful life is whatever *that person* determines is successful. If someone's dream is to buy some land in the Montana mountains, build a hut and live off the

"What determines a successful life is whatever that person determines is successful."

-Dave Mammano

land and they go and do it, then they're successful. That's what they wanted to do and they had the fortitude to do it. My version of success is having a business that allows me to help people build their future and also balance a wonderful family life. Do I need to make five million a year? No, but I want to make some money and be able to support my family. In the first few years of the magazine, did I have a little less sleep and a little more stress? Yes, but I didn't have a family yet, either. Success is having the fortitude to chase your dream and make it happen.

M: Campus Calm believes that you must surround yourself with positive people to maintain a happy and successful life. Could you share a few stories of how others have helped you create the life of your dreams? How can students learn to ignore the naysayers of the world, whether they be friends, family members or acquaintances in the supermarket?

D: Part of success is breaking up with friends who are not going to help you get there. You will have some negative friends who will not be happy for you as you succeed. They will start to be an anchor on your success if you stick with them. I know it's not easy but you just need to dump them. You need to stop returning their calls and going out with them because they're not helping you.

I have a lot of friends. If I have a friend who is not helping me be the person I want to be or is an anchor to my success, they're gone. You have to surround yourself with people who inspire you, encourage or support you and are happy for you. A lot of people can't do that because they get jealous. They don't want to see you succeed, so they try to sabotage you. If friends are draining your energy and you're getting nothing out of the relationships, then why are you still friends with them?

M: What if it's one or more family members?

D: You need to sit down with them and have a frank discussion. If they're not responsive, you need to limit your time around them. They need to share in your happiness, and if they don't, that's their problem. My family was very supportive from the beginning. They thought I was a little crazy, but it was an excited crazy.

I think it's more realistic these days to be an entrepreneur. The days where your dad would work at Kodak or another company for life are over. There are more chances and opportunities to own a business. With the Internet, anyone can start a Website and give it a try. There are a lot fewer barriers to entry these days. Frankly, a lot of smart young people are out there today, and they have the confidence to give it a shot.

M: Do you agree that happiness and success lie within your ability to focus inward and listen to what you want? How does a student go about learning to be authentic and to live authentically?

D: You have to be happy first. You're not going to be good for anyone else unless you're good first. Take care of yourself first and then you can do wonders for other people. As a teen and in my early twenties, I was the guy who tried to make everyone happy. A lot of times, I found myself

"Taking care of your emotional needs, getting sleep, exercising and eating well—that's not decadence or excess."

-Dave Mammano

exhausted. I appeared outwardly happy, but I felt absent. It eventually occurred to me, "Screw that! What about Dave?" Without being selfish, I thought of ways to make myself happy first. Bill Cosby says, "The definition of misery is trying to make everyone else around you happy." Taking care of your emotional needs, getting sleep, exercising and eating well—that's not decadence or excess. Taking part in activities or careers that fulfill you as a person isn't selfish. And if you do that, you're going to have a ton more energy for other people, anyway.

M: Campus Calm encourages students to envision a picture of success that would make them happy and then to work to achieve it. We also warn students not to be afraid to change that picture of success as they grow and learn new things. Could you share a personal story of how you changed your picture of success based on a new experience?

D: Starting my business was the one big thing that changed my life. I finally felt totally alive in every cell of my body. When I first started the magazine, I wanted to have a successful Rochester, New York magazine. Then I got bored so I brought it to Buffalo and Syracuse. Then I got bored so I expanded to all of New York State. So my definition of success kept moving. My 10-year goal for *Next Step* online is to have five million registered users. You set a goal and then when you get bored you move that goal higher.

M: How do you maintain a balance between planning for the future and having it completely mapped out so that it doesn't leave any room for spontaneity?

D: I use my team here at *Next Step* because if it were up to me, I would be on my tenth idea of the week already. I used to move way too fast, and a couple of years ago I was driving my team nuts. They told me that I had to slow down the treadmill because even though I had great ideas, they hadn't finished the ideas from the previous year. I rely on my team to keep me in check because otherwise I can be quite manic.

M: How did you find the courage to make some mistakes?

D: Most people are conservative and scared. I think it's a human trait that's taught by people who believe it themselves. The entrepreneurs are the ones who don't believe it. It's a good thing that not everyone thinks like us, because if they did there would be a lot more competition.

M: Campus Calm believes that creativity is the key behind any successful endeavor, whether it be perfecting your painter's stroke, giving a winning sales pitch or developing the latest computer software program. Do you think the word *creativity* is too often seen as only synonymous with "creative" careers such as writing, acting, dancing or painting? Doesn't any path to success require creativity?

D: Absolutely, you can be creative in many ways without being an artist or actress. The people who will stand out are a little bit more creative than the average person. If you're an accountant, a great way to be a better accountant is to be a little more creative with your clients.* Creativity is going to be the thing that separates you from the average people, regardless of what career you're in.

M: What does the word *creativity* mean to you?

D: Finding a way to do it differently and better. Finding a way to be unique. I'm not a painter. If we get an order here at *Next Step*, no matter who it is, I will personally e-mail the company and thank them for the order. That one letter is very creative because no one else is doing stuff like that. Customers think it's a big deal to have the CEO send them a thank you e-mail. That's creative. It's finding a creative solution to help you stand out.

M: How can students learn to hone their creativity?

D: I would say, "What are some things you want to do with your life?" If they say, "I want to be a lawyer," I say, "You're 16 years old—what can you be doing right now to learn about that career?" They'll say, "I could get an internship or a part-time job." I say, "Sure, how are you going to do that? How are you going to make yourself stand out?" When I was in college and I was looking for a job, I made a cereal box with my résumé on one side and my picture on the other side. What can students today do? How about if they go through the phone book and start calling lawyers and

---

* *But not too creative, says the IRS!*

say, "Hi, I'm Suzie Smith, I'm 16 years old from such-and-such high school and I'm thinking about becoming a lawyer. Could I come talk to you for a half hour?" Most adults would be honored that some kid was thinking about their career. That's creative.

M: Some students read about the top 10 fastest-growing careers and decide they'll give one of those a try instead of focusing first on where their passions lie. How important is passion in realizing a happy and successful life? Is passion for your chosen career as important as, say, a polished résumé, a perfect GPA or a name-brand college? Why?

D: Everyone who works at *Next Step* went to a state school. Especially with undergraduate work, the name-brand diploma doesn't mean anything. I've known a lot of idiots who went to nice expensive schools. At any school, the skills can be taught, but the attitude can't.

M: Campus Calm believes that one major part of living a happy and successful life is ditching your inner perfectionist. Could you share a personal story of how this statement was proven true in your life? Have you ever tried to be perfect at something and ended up losing yourself in the process?

D: Going back to my business, it's great to make mistakes. That's how you learn. If you're a perfectionist, you're petrified of making a mistake. That puts you in a prison because if you're not taking chances, then you're not growing as a person. Once I decided that it was okay to make mistakes in my business because I could learn from them, then it was okay. Being a perfectionist limits you, and I don't see how it could be good for your health. I make a lot of mistakes every day, but I'm trying, and I don't repeat the same mistake twice. Jump into the pool with a huge cannon ball! Am I going to be 80 years old sitting on my rocking chair and regretting the things I didn't try because I was scared I would fail? No, that's the failure. You're failing if you're trying to be a perfectionist because you're not growing.

"Am I going to be 80 years old sitting on my rocking chair and regretting the things I didn't try because I was scared I would fail? No, that's the failure."

-Dave Mammano

Appendix B
Overcoming Academic Perfectionism

Q&A with Hilary Silver, LCSW, Mental Health Expert, Campus Calm

I want students to understand that ditching your inner perfectionist takes time and effort. You can't just tell the inner critic—who gives you hell when you get a B on a paper or you make a mistake when trying something new—to shut up and be done with it. There is no quick fix. I'm learning how to ditch my own inner perfectionist every day. I still struggle with it from time to time. I also want students to understand that every person's situation is unique. You can use my experience as inspiration to help guide you, but you cannot follow my exact steps to leave perfection in the dust. You must assess where you are and take the steps that are right for you. That's why I decided to talk with Hilary Silver, Campus Calm's Mental Health Expert.

Maria: Does ditching our inner perfectionist start with monitoring our internal self-talk?

Hilary: Yes, monitoring our self-talk is an important first step because we need to get in touch with our inner dialogue and know what we're saying to ourselves all day long. From there we may begin to see patterns of thought that are damaging to our mental health. Correcting negative self-

talk is one part of healing; the other parts are to understand the purpose these thoughts are serving and to accept
that they're just thoughts, not necessarily truths. And it's
important for the perfectionist to hear that it takes time
to work this out—patience is critical and baby steps are
still steps. A good mantra might sound like, "I am who I
am. This is where I am right now, and it's taken me years
to get to this point in my life. Anything I can do to make
myself evolve in my consciousness is good. I give myself
credit for even being aware of my inner perfectionist."

M: That's an interesting point that you just brought up because it
reminds me of my own experience. I had to realize that I wasn't
just going to turn around and have perfect mental health. I
wasn't going to ditch my own inner perfectionist and find peace
in a perfect way.

H: That's right. Self-awareness or mindfulness is a practice, and it
requires commitment. It can take a lifetime to really understand
who you are and to be at peace with who you are. We constantly
figure out which parts of ourselves are changeable and which
parts are always going to be there. For the parts of ourselves
that we can't change, we need to learn how to be at peace with
that. We are who we are because of the earliest imprints on our
lives; therefore, identifying and replacing unhealthy, damaging
thoughts and beliefs is a process. So yes, we need to tune into
our own self-talk. But it's important to accept where we are in
the present moment and be patient with ourselves while we em-
bark upon this journey.

It's interesting that you used the word *perfect* to describe your desired state of mental health because another piece of this discussion is to understand that perfectionist thinking is a type of cognitive distortion, which means that it's a manner of thinking that's twisted just a bit or is irrational. To think that you can be perfect is irrational because there's no such thing as perfect, not in nature and certainly not in the mind of a perfectionist. It's a bit like trying to hit a moving target: nearly impossible. An example of this type of cognitive distortion is the "if/then" syndrome where the thought is something like, "If I get an A on this next exam, then I will be perfect," or, "Once I win that award, I will be happy." Except that once such a goal is achieved, the next goal is identified, and only upon that next success will you be "perfect." And then the cycle continues.

 "To think that you can be perfect is irrational because there's no such thing as perfect."
-Hilary Silver

M: So would the first step be tuning in to our own self-talk and the type of things that we say to ourselves? For example, if a student doesn't get an A on a paper, she might think, "Oh my God, I'm so stupid. I'm never going to get into a good college, or get a good job, or be successful." So does it start with maybe realizing that, "Okay, this is what I'm saying to myself." Then what might be the very next step? Might it be to go to counseling? Might it be to read a book on perfectionism?

H: There are a lot of things you can do. I always think counseling is great because it's like taking a class on yourself, like having a personal trainer at the gym or a nutritionist for your dietary needs. If counseling isn't an option, there are many great self-help books on the market.

Briefly, an example of replacing negative self-talk (cognitive distortions) would be to respond to your identified negative thought with, "Okay, what are three alternative ways I can look at this situation? So I didn't get an A on this paper. Did I give it my best? I think I did, but I was a little distracted because I went out drinking the night before." Or, "I didn't get an A on this paper, but I got an A on every other paper since or before. Does that really mean that I'm doomed for life because of one B? What is the absolute worst thing that will happen to me because of this B?"

I think that this practice of combating the negative thoughts with numerous other perspectives on the very same situation will help you see that you're choosing this one perspective that doesn't feel very good. You will learn that there are, in fact, many other ways to see the same situation.

M: This flows directly into my next question. We are what we think, and we get to choose our self-thoughts. No one sticks a gun to our heads and forces us to believe anything. How can students assess whether their self-talk is in alignment with who they wish/believe themselves to be?

H: We do get to choose our thoughts and beliefs about ourselves. But this awareness comes later in life, and until that time, such thoughts and beliefs aren't part of the consciousness. Once that realization is made, the real work begins: deciding if those thoughts are in alignment with who we wish to be. And often the most difficult part is figuring out who we do wish to be. It can really be an emotional and existential struggle when there's a disconnect between someone's thoughts and their hopes or their reality. I think this is the best time for self–reflection and/or counseling because you're becoming insightful and are ready for the change that's about to happen.

M: Some students may wish themselves to be strong, independent and resilient people. But then their own self-talk is not in alignment with those goals. So is one of the steps just realizing this misalignment?

H: Yes, but even more, I think it's important for students to have realistic goals and expectations. It takes time to embody strength and resilience. We're all on a journey to becoming the person we wish to be; patience with yourself and trust in the growth process are key to self-acceptance and to being content and happy in the moment.

> "It takes time to embody strength and resilience."
>
> -Hilary Silver

M: In school, we often focus on our deficits. If we get an A in one subject and a C in another, everyone focuses in on that C. Instead of cultivating our strengths we tend to focus on our shortcomings. Is that part of it?

H: That's absolutely a big part of it. Many people focus on their perceived shortcomings instead of acknowledging their strengths and triumphs. Or they may minimize the value of their strengths while giving more weight to the areas they believe are their deficits. This is actually another example of cognitive distortions.

Somehow, that focus needs to shift to a more balanced view of reality. Getting a C in one subject might be more valuable than getting an A in another because that class may have been much more challenging. So a healthier perspective would be pride in meeting that challenge instead of condemning the C.

M: If the first step is being aware of self-thoughts, how can students next learn how to take control of their thoughts and internalize the sentiments of Eleanor Roosevelt, who said, "No one can make you feel inferior without your consent."

H: Your self-thoughts are what bubble up to the surface. The deepest core beliefs fuel those thoughts. What you believe about yourself is what you offer up to the world, which will be all that we know of you. If you believe deep down inside that you're inferior, then you will teach people to treat you as if you are inferior, and people may even be compelled to believe you are.

M: So many of the students who contact me have come to define themselves through their grades. I was the oldest of four kids and being the smart one, the good student, was how I defined myself. When you strip that away, it's very scary, because you then say, "Who am I?" We cling to the one role by which we have come to define ourselves.

H: Yes, but that's not giving yourself credit for the infinite other wonderful qualities that you have within you. Just being "the smart one" is very limiting and fails to recognize that you are a human being with a multitude of characteristics and experiences that make you the unique and complicated individual you are.

M: How can you be in tune with your inner critic and garner the necessary lessons it may be trying to teach you while still not allowing that critic to prevent you from taking new chances?

H: It's important to listen and hear that critic because sometimes that critic is your consciousness guiding you to be that person you want to be. Other times, that critic is judgmental and irrational (cognitive distortions). Hear the critic, but then stop and evaluate before you speak, act or make a decision. Pause. If you hold your tongue for just a few moments, your response will be different, and you won't be acting on impulse with your critic fueling your feelings. Time offers us a unique opportunity to gain perspective.

M: If a student is struggling with all these issues, maybe the advice would be that they go to their campus counseling centers. Sometimes perfectionist students don't realize that they're in trouble. They might rationalize it away by saying, "Okay, so I'm a little bit upset, I'm a little bit grade obsessed, but at least I'm not failing out of my classes. I'm not doing drugs; I'm not drinking excessively. I'm not like *that* person. I'm not really in trouble." What would you say to that?

H: I would say, "Do you have to be in a lot of trouble before you get help?" If you were falling behind in a class, would you wait to get help until you have an F? A better approach would be to say, "I'm not quite getting this concept. I'm going to ask for help before I get too far behind." I would ask the student who says she's not that person who needs help, "What does that mean? Do you believe it's wrong to know what you need and to get help?" Knowing when to get help demonstrates self-awareness. Getting help takes courage.

M: Is it hard for a perfectionist to admit that he or she might need help because that's saying, "I'm not perfect if I'm struggling"?

H: Yes, absolutely. But I would say, "Take an inventory of yourself and be honest." Am I really happy? Am I at peace? Am I content? On a day-to-day basis, am I struggling? How do I feel about myself? Can I give myself a break? Is it better to feign perfection or to achieve true happiness?

M: Any last words of wisdom?

H: Strive for a kinder, gentler, more self-loving approach to who you are right now in the moment. Overachieving students want it all and they want it all now. You want to be perfect and there is no room for mistakes. Be okay with where you are right now, and know that it's a necessary step for where you will be going.

> "Be okay with where you are right now, and know that it's a necessary step for where you will be going."
> -Hilary Silver

Appendix C
Maria's Mailbag

Below is a sampling of the kind of letters* I receive every day
from stressed-out high school and college students around the
world. They're responding to my article**, "Summa Cum Laude &
Valedictorian: Are They Worth It?" Together, we can all learn how
to transform the college experience to include personal wellness
while still living up to our full potential and greatness. That's our
Campus Calm Community promise to you!

Live your bliss,

Maria

---

* *Last names and schools in some cases have been removed to protect students'*
privacy

** **www.campuscalm.com/summa**

Hi Maria,

I stumbled upon your Website while surfing the Internet, and I almost cried when I read your biography. It felt like I was reading my own. I am a college junior majoring in biology with a minor in chemistry. I make myself sick if I receive anything less than an A on tests. I put my entire self-worth and identity into my academic accomplishments, trying to prove to everyone that I'm talented. I'm an obsessive perfectionist when it comes to school. Your story really inspired me and I love your Website.

Sincerely,

Shelly

———— ◎ ◎ ◎ ————

Maria,

I just came upon your site. I too graduated summa cum laude, *having returned to school to get my degree in architecture. I never realized that I would graduate with honors, but always felt that if I didn't nearly kill myself, I would fail the class … ha, crazy!*

Also, since so few people actually graduate with that level of honor, some employers are put off by it. So, good luck with your work of educating young people. They should have a varied experience in college.

m.e.doris

———— ◎ ◎ ◎ ————

Good evening, Maria!

I am a 20-year-old college student from the Philippines, and I just read your wonderful article about graduating summma cum laude. I just have two questions for you regarding this subject.

1. Is it really possible to make it as summa cum laude without losing oneself in the process? (Meaning you won't become insanely exhausted after four years.)

2. What advice would you give to those students (myself included) who are dead serious about graduating at the top of the class?

Thanks,

Karen

———— ⑥ ⑥ ⑥ ————

Maria,

I read your article about graduating summa cum laude. I also have a passion to be perfect but am not always (perfect). We're always our worst critic aren't we!!! I'm taking five classes and run my own construction business. I feel like my head's in a vise at times, but I seem to manage it all. I feel like when I'm out for the summer I'm just wasting time. But I read your story and saw myself in it. How did you ever shake that feeling? I can't seem to.

Darren

——— ⊚ ⊚ ⊚ ———

Maria,

*I found your article on the pursuit of perfection quite help-
ful and something that I can really relate to. During law
school I worked myself to a standstill in an attempt to
achieve* summa cum laude *honors. After achieving this, I
was awarded a scholarship to study in the U.S. During my
second semester in the U.S., both my mind and body finally
reached breaking point and I ended up in a mental health
facility for two weeks. I was diagnosed with bipolar disorder, and I had apparently suffered a manic episode.*

*This was the scariest thing I have ever endured; I was con-
vinced that I was going to die. It's been six months since my
diagnosis, and I have had no reoccurring episodes. I think
my breakdown could be attributed to my pushing myself
over the edge to achieve perfection in my studies—while
other aspects of my life were spinning completely out of control. I could not believe it when I was sitting in a room filled
with alcoholics, drug addicts and prisoners, but I realized
that in many ways I was not very different from any of those
people. So I am writing this to thank you for sharing your
experience online so that others can be enlightened and can
hopefully escape having to learn things the hard way.*

Kind Regards,

Lisa

——— ⊚ ⊚ ⊚ ———

Maria,

I just read your article and it was as if I wrote it myself. Your story exactly mirrors what I am currently doing to myself. Nothing is ever good enough; even a 94 percent is disappointing. I always feel I should have done this, or I could have done better, etc. I have gotten to the point that I'm now taking medication to help with the anxiety. I don't know why I do this to myself. I'm sitting here afraid to complete this huge project worth 50 percent of my grade because I'm afraid it won't be "good enough." Right now, I feel completely 100 percent burned out and fresh out of any creative ideas. Why? I have a 3.95 GPA and now I'm terrified of "blowing it." AHAHAH. How can I give this up and not let it rule my life?

Sincerely,

Carrie

Thanks for sharing your story, Maria. My name is Austin and I am a senior undergraduate. I experienced something similar to what you described in being stressed out by perfectionism. I think it's important for college students today to seriously evaluate where they find their self-worth and to question what is most important for them. Out of curiosity, did you go through any spiritual transformation during this time? I know for myself that my explanation of faith played a key role in my "liberation" from stress related to perfectionism.

——— ⊚ ⊚ ⊚ ———

*I just wanted to tell you how much I appreciated your piece,
"In Pursuit of Perfection," on the Campus Calm Website.
During high school and my first year in college, I suffered
some of the psychological damages from overstressing about
everything, from academics to eating. I have been working
to try to regain control over those aspects of my life, and
your article helped to put some things into perspective. It's
unfortunate that so many students feel such immense pressure to be perfect at everything. Thank you for making a
difference; your article is a good wake-up call.*

Christopher

——— ⊚ ⊚ ⊚ ———

Hi Maria,

*I would just like to write you and say thank you so much
for creating this Website. It's about time I've found it! I've
been a stressed-out high school student for three full years
now, and the past year and a half I have also been going
to college. I keep my self very busy with school and always
strive to do my best. I used to be a lot worse than I am now.
After taking a college class where I was glad to get a C on a
test, I learned that you don't have to do great on everything.
Usually I try to get A's, but in that class I was just trying
to pass. It was probably one of the most difficult classes I
have ever been in, but I managed to pass it and learn that
good grades don't matter all that much, just as long as you*

are trying your hardest. Even though I know that, I still get over my head in work sometimes and stressed out.

Aubrey

Maria, I've gotta tell you, the class list comes out and shows who's on the top and you try so hard to be in the top 20. The top 15—all their averages are at least 100. Sometimes when I'm studying, I'll say, "I don't get this, I'll never remember this for the test. What about the SATs? I'll never get into college. I'll never be successful."

Rachel

Hello!

Normally I'm not one to e-mail folks out of the blue, but your articles on perfectionism in college were really spot-on with what I go through during my daily college grind. :) Today is the first day of my spring break and, more so than going on vacation or generally goofing off with friends, I was excited to not have any exams or assignments to stress over.

Unfortunately, I got an unpleasant surprise when I checked my midterm grades; of my 19-hour credit load, I got a B+ in one of my classes. Horror! I type that with sarcasm, but all the same I can still feel a familiar knot of stress growing in my stomach.

Never mind that a 19-hour load is a very strenuous course load. Never mind that many of my classes are in creative pursuits, all of which are subjective. Never mind that the B+ is for a photography class, and I've never held an SLR camera before mid-January. It's really, really frustrating. All I can think is, "Oh God, I'm going to lose my perfect 4.0. It's my junior year—why couldn't I hold out three more semesters?" Which, honestly, is ridiculous. But just because I'm cognizant of the fact that my mind is wired a bit funny doesn't mean that I know how to fix the break. (Not only that, but it's only mid-semester. I still have plenty of time to transform that B+ to an A. I just can't help but play the pessimist.)

I know that I'm naturally wired to be an overachiever. One incident that, today, I still can't believe: after being in a terrible car wreck and breaking my wrist bad enough to require surgery, I still typed my papers one-handed and turned them in early. Even after my professors kindly granted me a grace period.

I suppose all of my rambling is just to say: I feel you, man. It's good to know that I'm not so strange after all. I wish I could lighten my stress load—I still haven't figured that out—but your story definitely spoke to me. I'm trying to accept my faults. I'm trying to embrace my love of learning. Grades are just my sticking point.

-J. (Even after typing out my life's story, a little train of thought is still running through my head: "B+, B+ ... " Gah! :p)

Jessica, a college junior attending college in South Carolina

———— ⑥ ⑥ ⑥ ————

Hi Maria,

I have been dealing with anxiety and depression for four years now and have found this year to be especially difficult with the transition into my freshman year of college. My mom heard about your Website and thought that she would pass it along to me. When I first looked at it, I thought it was an interesting concept and signed up for the mailing list. I didn't really think much more about it after that. Probably a week later I was having a really rough day, I was homesick, stressed and down in the dumps when your newsletter popped up in my mailbox. It was one of the most encouraging sights just to know that there are people out there who are going through the same thing as me and who are struggling, as well. Your newsletter always comes at the perfect time, when I need it the most. Thanks for all your hard work in bringing awareness to stress and anxiety issues. Keep up the good work!

*name removed to protect the young woman's privacy

———— ⑥ ⑥ ⑥ ————

Dear Maria,

I just read your story about whether it's worth it to chase the summa cum laude *status. The story moved me. I too achieved that elusive 4.0, and in the end, I don't know if it was worth it. I gave up so much to be at the top, and it was a lonely place to be. The many nights that I rejected offers to go out and make friends made me a loner. The people who wanted to hang out with me were only there to copy my homework or wanted me to tutor them. When I tell people I have a 4.0, they're impressed at this seemingly impossible achievement, but I think it's quite overrated. I did it to prove to my parents that I was worthy of their admiration and love. I did it to prove that women can achieve the highest honors in a male dominated field (computer science). I also did it to prove to myself about my own self-worth.*

Today, I'm happier reaching for goals that are motivated by happiness. My type A personality still makes me inclined to be perfect, but I now know better how to strike a balance. I'm so glad you shared your summa experience with the world. You wrote the things that I could not express. I thought that all achievers just go through life achieving and never questioning, but then when I did question, I realized that there were many unanswerable questions. They weren't as easy as the tests that I aced in school. Kudos for your achievement. Sometimes all we need to know is that we're not alone and we're not the only ones feeling this way. Thank you for that.

Stephanie, college graduate, Drexel University

---- ⊚ ⊚ ⊚ ----

Hi Maria,

Just dropping by to let you know that this Campus Calm

thing's a HUGE help to me, and I'm sure many others.

It's such a great tool to get me through an insanely hectic junior year ahead. So, how much is doing TOO much, exactly? Because I've read stuff on "downsides of being an overachiever" and I'm not quite sure if I need to worry about being too crazy.

My day starts around 6:45 a.m., and in the fall my schedule will include: AP Biology, AP U.S. History, Honors English, Honors Pre Calculus, Spanish, ASB, Volleyball and Advanced Theatre. Sometimes I feel like there's never enough time in the day to get everything done. I'm a HUGE procrastinator, quite a perfectionist and slightly sleep-deprived. But somehow, I manage to pull off a 4.6 GPA.

But I don't know. At what point will I explode?! I mean with SATs coming up and arghh ... . Oh and I'm thinking of starting the Filipino club at my school.

Gosh! Is all this worth it??? Others get by just fine with regular classes ... and it's not like they're NOT going to college.

Anyway, thanks again ...

Campus Calm all the way!

Michelle

Hi Maria,

Balancing academics with the other areas of your life is the absolute key to sanity and good mental health. I just gradu-ated summa cum laude *from college. While it does feel great to know all the hard work paid off, I wonder whether all the forgone opportunities to go out, attend movies or live events on campus, or just spend quality time with friends were re-ally worth three Latin words on my diploma.*

Joseph Felix, recent college graduate, University of Califor-nia, Los Angeles

Maria,

I don't believe that anyone can achieve a high honor without some kind of stress. No matter what you want to achieve in life, there will be stress along the way. The only thing you can do is find ways to relieve it. Because if you let the stress store inside you, you'll have problems. It's okay to get stressed sometimes; just don't let it overpower you.

I always wished that I could have worked harder in high school so I could at least have been on the Director's List (honor roll). My obsession with the honor roll made me feel like I was less of a student and even less of a person. The strange thing is that no one pushed me to be on the honor roll but me. I was killing myself. All I can say is, "Don't be so damn hard on yourself. RELAX."

Jasmine Reynolds, college freshman, Saint Mary's College of California

——— ⑥ ⑥ ⑥ ———

Maria,

I recently graduated summa cum laude. *I googled* summa cum laude *and up popped your story. I loved it. What you went through matches how I feel: too worried about doing well to stop and enjoy. I printed the story for my teenage daughter, still in high school. She screamed, "Yes, that's me!" By going through it, you know what the stress is like. It's nice to know someone else has gone through what we're going through. I'm glad you're reaching out and helping others. Your service is needed more than you know.*

Thank you, Maria,

Robin

——— ⑥ ⑥ ⑥ ———

Dear Maria,

I'm a junior in high school and I just can't seem to maintain my high expectation for myself in all of my classes. I have absolutely no free time on the weekends, mostly due to AP classes and a lot of projects. In my classes I feel that I have to make A's, and in AP classes if I get anything less than the full 5 points, I've wasted my time. I'm constantly worrying about how I'll do on the AP exam. I also feel that my GPA isn't high enough, and I want to get it to the point where my class rank is higher (currently 32nd), but my parents keep saying that a 3.94 is great. What should I do? Please help me!!!

*name removed to protect the young man's privacy

———— ⊚ ⊚ ⊚ ————

Maria,

I came upon your Website while I was looking for the defini-tion of summa cum laude*! As an almost 50-year-old woman who will graduate in April 2009 with my BSN, I completely understood what you and the many others were feeling while striving for that elusive "with highest honors." Thirty years ago, I was in an associates nursing program with a 2.5 GPA. I was grateful just to have gotten out of school. Now, I feel that I have 28 years of experience behind me and that I must be "perfect." I have a 3.9 GPA (my only B: Sta-tistics). I was devastated and annoyed when I actually got an 88 on a final paper in Nursing Research (bringing my grade down to a 92). With only my classroom participation grade to count on, I could actually get an A- (gaaaasp).*

It goes to show you that age doesn't matter. Stress, anxiety and perfectionism do not discriminate based on age. I will be reading your book (then I will give it to my 20 year-old who is in college!).

Mary McDermott, RN

———— ⊚ ⊚ ⊚ ————

Maria,

I just wanted to say thank you for writing the article on perfectionism. As a nontraditional college student who has had an obsession with making straight A's since the fifth grade, I can relate with your story of feeling mostly sadness when you've reached your goal. As a valedictorian of my class in 1999, I suffered from severe burnout and dragged myself through a year of college before quitting. To add insult to injury, I got a B in a class that would have been a sure A if I had not been so depressed and missed out on class discussion points.

Now, I'm back in school and taking prerequisite courses for a highly competitive program, and, after less than a year, I'm already on the track to burnout. Furthermore, due to trick questions on a series of true and false tests, I fear I may get another B in an otherwise easy class. I know I shouldn't get so upset, but since I neglect friends, family and fun just to do my best, I feel like a complete failure who has sacrificed too much for too little when I fall short of my goals.

I know I'll always struggle with these feelings to some extent, but hearing your story helps me feel less alone because I've really only met one other person whom I can relate to about this.

Sincerely,

Michelle

———— ◎ ◎ ◎ ————

Maria,

After checking out your Website, I really felt compelled to e-mail you. I really can relate to all the students about the anxiety and stress of receiving perfect grades, although I am 28 years old now.

When I was in high school I always received A's. If I occasionally received a B I was so disappointed in myself because I knew I was letting my father down. I eventually dropped out of high school because I began to suffer from depression and I couldn't take the stress anymore. I felt like a failure. I then went on to have two children and decided I need to get my GED and get back into school.

I started at a community college and my GPA was never below a 3.75. But the stress and anxiety I dealt with definitely had a negative impact on my family life. When I would receive my grades, there was never a sense of accomplishment, just a feeling of relief that I made it through another semester. I eventually went on antidepressants and sleeping pills to help with stress. I then transferred to a university last fall (2008). Again, the anxiety and stress of trying to get good grades became so overwhelming I had my doctor "up" my medication. When I received my final grades I was so disappointed! My GPA was a 3.5. I thought to myself, I will never be able to get into the National Honor Society. So that is where I stand right now. I am already having anxiety over the next semester and am trying to raise my GPA.

Fortunately, your Website really got me thinking. My grades do not define who I am. So what if I don't graduate with honors? It doesn't make me any less of a mother, sister,

daughter, friend. I am still a dedicated worker with ambi-
tions. I just really want to thank you for your Website.

*name removed to protect the young woman's privacy

Dear Maria,

I am a junior premed and psychology major. I am e-mailing
you because I want you to know that Campus Calm is
amazing. Every time I visit your Website, without fail, I
start bawling my eyes out—the articles give me an incred-
ible relief and understanding that I haven't experienced
anywhere else. I have suffered from perfectionism and anxi-
ety for as long as I can remember, and I have grown to hate
college as my academic and work stresses continue to pile
up. Despite a 3.99 GPA, I am miserable and feel completely
overwhelmed by the demands that I continue to put on my-
self. Although I have seen a counselor, she actually told me
that it was good to keep up my goal of straight A's!

Your site is the only one I have seen that conveys realistic
expectations that actually consider and acknowledge the
importance of a young woman's health and personal life.
I wish that more professors and professionals fully under-
stood the increasing demands and problems of perfection-
ism among young women of this generation, and what a
miserable prison it can be.

Your happiness and hope inspire me to work toward my
own. Please keep up your fantastic work, and thank you.

*name removed to protect the young woman's privacy

Appendix D

Campus Calm U Recommends

Maria's picks

Books

⊚ Adderholdt, Miriam, PhD and Jan Goldberg. *Perfectionism: What's Bad About Being Too Good?* Free Spirit Publishing, 1999.

> When I was finally ready to ditch my inner perfectionist, this was the first book I found at the library. Boy was I glad I did! A must-read for any student looking to break free from the chains of perfectionism.

⊚ Levine, Madeline, PhD *The Price of Privilege: How Parental Pressure and Material Advantage Are Creating a Generation of Disconnected and Unhappy Kids.* HarperCollins, 2006.

> An insightful book for parents and young adult children about how our materialistic culture can adversely affect children and the struggling parents trying to raise them. Money can't buy happiness, but can retail therapy effectively feed an unhappy consumerist-driven culture?

◎ Logan, Alan, ND and Valori Treloar. *The Clear Skin Diet.* Cumberland House Publishing, 2007.

> I included this book as a resource because it contains extensive scientific research about how stress affects our entire bodies, including our skin. *The Clear Skin* Diet really isn't about dieting at all. The authors argue that no one pill, potion or cream will magically heal our bodies. Instead, eating whole, nutritious foods, managing stress, exercising and infusing joy into our lives will help us look better from the inside out ... and heal unsightly blemishes that we hate so much!

◎ Pope, Denise Clark. *Doing School: How We Are Creating a Generation of Stressed-Out, Materialistic, and Miseducated Students.* Yale University Press, 2001.

> *Doing School* reminded me of what happens when you view education not as an end in itself, but solely as a means to move up the success ladder. A must-read for anyone trying to appreciate learning for the sake of learning.

◎ Quindlen, Anna. *Being Perfect.* Random House, 2005.

> My favorite short book written by my favorite author. Campus Calm might not exist if I had never been introduced to her wonderful words.

◎ Robbins, Alexandra. *The Overachievers: The Secret Lives of Driven Kids.* Hyperion, 2006.

> Journalist Alexandra Robbins delivers a page-turning narrative that explores how our high-stakes educational culture has spiraled out of control. Issues covered include the student and teacher cheating epidemic, over-testing, sports rage, the

black market for study drugs and a college admissions process so cutthroat that some students are driven to depression and suicide because of a B.

⊚ Siebert, Al, PhD and Karr, Mary, MS. *The Adult Student's Guide to Survival & Success* Sixth Edition. Practical Psychology Press, 2008.

Adult students need some Campus Calm too! If you're struggling to learn how to balance school with work and family and want some tips on how to be resilient in non-stop change, this is a must-read for you.

Websites

⊚ Active Minds on Campus **www.activemindsoncampus.org**

Active Minds is the nation's only peer-to-peer organization dedicated to raising awareness about mental health among college students. The organization serves as the young adult voice in mental health advocacy on over two hundred college campuses nationwide.

⊚ Alfie Kohn **www.alfiekohn.org**

An insightful critic of education's fixation on grades and test scores. Author of books like *The Homework Myth, What Does It Mean to Be Well Educated?* and *Punished by Rewards,* Kohn is for the brave-hearted looking for a mean debate on education, parenting and the state of our nation's children.

◎ Brad Sachs, PhD **www.bradsachs.com**

Author of *When No One Understands: Letters to a Teenager On Life, Loss, and the Hard Road to Adulthood* and *The Good Enough Teen: How to Raise Adolescents with Love and Acceptance (Despite How Impossible They Can Be).*

◎ Challenge Success **www.challengesuccess.org**

Challenge Success is an expanded version of the Stanford University School of Education SOS: Stressed-Out Students Project. With a rise in recent years in the number of students seeking mental health services, an increase in cheating behavior in school and students' constant worry about academic achievement, Challenge Success is committed to endorsing a vision of success that emphasizes character, health, independence, connection, creativity, enthusiasm and achievement.

◎ College Parents of America **www.collegeparents.org**

College Parents of America is a national membership association serving current and future college parents.

◎ Come Recommended **www.comerecommended.com**

Launched by Heather Huhman, Campus Calm's Job Search Expert, Come Recommended is an exclusive online community connecting the best internship and entry-level candidates with the best employers.

Come Recommended will help you stress less during your internship or entry-level job search in the following three ways:

1. Candidate members must have graduated no longer than one year ago. That means no more competing against people who aren't truly entry-level.

2. Everyone in the community must have three recommendations before they are allowed to interact with you, and that includes employers. These recommendations are displayed clearly on every profile. No more wondering whether or not your potential employer "comes recommended" by those who have worked there in the past.

3. Once accepted into the community, you will have the ability to chat directly with hiring managers through the site. You can initiate a conversation with them, and vice versa. If you visit an employer's profile and you like what you see, send a chat request and tell them. Even better, you can request an informational video interview—no need to travel to them!

© Forget Perfect **www.forgetperfect.com**

Website of Lisa Earle McLeod, syndicated humor columnist and author of *Forget Perfect: Finding joy, meaning, and satisfaction in the life you've already got and the YOU you already are* and *Finding Grace When You Can't Even Find Clean Underwear.* If you want a good laugh and some motivation to ditch your inner perfectionist, you'll want to check out this site.

⊚ Half of Us **www.halfofus.com**

> From the Half of Us Website: Did you know that nearly half of all college students reported feeling so depressed that they couldn't function during the last school year? Through Half of Us, mtvU and The Jed Foundation want to initiate a public dialogue to raise awareness about the prevalence of mental health issues on campus and connect students to the appropriate resources to get help.

⊚ Happiness Makeover **www.happinessmakeover.com**

> Take the Happiness Makeover quiz and sign up to receive a daily happiness booster in your e-mail. In the words of M.J. Ryan, author of *The Happiness Makeover*, "Teach yourself to be happy and enjoy every day."

⊚ Health Journeys **www.healthjourneys.com**

> Guided imagery CDs and tapes, therapy and meditation. This Website offers a fantastic supply of relaxation CDs and tapes on stress management, insomnia, testing anxiety and depression. They even have a tape to help you quit smoking. Audio MP3s are available in some cases as well.

⊚ "High Achievers—What Price are They Paying?"
   www.school.familyeducation.com

> This article, written by my friend Carleton Kendrick EdM, LCSW, also inspired me to create Campus Calm.

◎ Jean Kilbourne **www.jeankilbourne.com**

> Lecturer, activist and author of *Can't Buy My Love: How Advertising Changes the Way We Think and Feel.* I first discovered Jean Kilbourne when I was a junior in college. As a fellow writer, Jean taught me how persuasive words could be. I felt a profound responsibility to use my talents for the greater good after reading her book. Her book also helped to make me an obnoxious copywriter—when I worked in the advertising department at *The Buffalo News,* a sales rep wanted me to craft a headline for a tanning salon with a Christmas angle for their holiday gift guide. So I presented him this headline: "Even Santa Gets Skin Cancer." Truth in advertising—what a concept!

◎ JED Foundation—Strengthening the Mental Health Safety Net for College Students **www.jedfoundation.org**

> Learn about the many excellent resources and programs designed to help college students find information on the signs and symptoms of depression and to encourage help-seeking.

◎ Lindsey Pollak **www.lindseypollak.com**

> Lindsey is Campus Calm's new Networking Expert. She is the author of the popular career advice book for college students and recent grads, *Getting from College to Career: 90 Things to Do Before You Join the Real World* (HarperCollins, April 2007) and co-author with Diane K. Danielson of *The Savvy Gal's Guide to Online Networking (Or, What Would Jane Austen Do?).*

◉ Massage on the Go USA **www.massageonthegousa.com**

Founded in 1996 by Meredith and Michael Gansrow, both licensed massage therapists, Massage On The Go USA is the
leading massage therapy practice catering to the U.S. college
market. The Gansrows realize that students who learn how
to manage stress early tend to stay in school and flourish, as
well.

◉ National Center for Fair & Open Testing **www.fairtest.org**

FairTest works to end the misuses and flaws of standardized
testing and to ensure that evaluation of students, teachers
and schools is fair, open, valid and educationally beneficial.
I chose to include this Website here because of its list of over
815 four-year colleges that do not use the SAT I or ACT to
admit substantial numbers of bachelor degree applicants.
Check out the searchable list of schools.

◉ National Mental Health Awareness Campaign **www.nostigma.org**

Committed to battling the stigma, shame, and myths surrounding mental disorders that prevent so many people from
getting the help they need. Read about mental health myths,
warning signs facts and find out how you can get involved.

◉ "Overachievers Find Success Comes with a Psychological Price"
researchnews.osu.edu/archive/achiever.htm

I was first introduced to the research conducted by Dr. Robert Arkin on overachievers in 2002. His research fascinated
me because I did much better in college than my SAT scores
would have predicted. In concurrence with Dr. Arkin's re-

search findings, my overachieving ways unfortunately came with a psychological price.

◎ Progressive U **www.progressiveu.org**

Connect with other students who are committed to thinking, blogging and debating about more than the latest party or Sunday morning hangover.

◎ Resiliency Center **www.resiliencycenter.com**

Website of Al Siebert, PhD, author of *The Resiliency Advantage: Master Change, Thrive Under Pressure, and Bounce Back from Setbacks.* Take the resiliency quiz, "How Resilient Are You?" on his Website. I scored average on his quiz last year, but I've upped my score in the past twelve months. Track your progress over the next year.

◎ University Chic **www.universitychic.com**

University Chic is an online magazine written for and by university women across the nation and world. I serve as a College Stress Expert on their site. Let me know what topics you want covered!

◎ Young Investors Guide **www.younginvestorsguide.com**

The Website of Monte Malhotra, Stanford University college student, economics major, young entrepreneur and investment guru. Learn the steps to investing your money as a college student so you can set up a secure financial future.

◎ Young Money **www.youngmoney.com**

Student loans, car payments, credit card debt. Worried about bankrupting yourself before your 25th birthday? Learn how to take charge over your financial future now and empower yourself with the ability to make choices to help secure a less stressful twentysomething experience.

Yoga, Meditation & Fitness

◎ AM/PM Yoga for Beginners **www.gaiam.com**

A top pick in my DVD collection. Led by Rodney Yee, *AM Yoga* is about 20 minutes and *PM Yoga* (led by Patricia Walden) runs about 25 minutes. They're both fantastic segments that help me relieve stress. Some would consider it a bonus: you get to see Rodney Yee in Speedos. ☺

◎ Daily Dose of Dharma with Danica McKellar
www.dailydoseofdharma.com

One of my favorite Yoga/Meditation DVDs. Stretch your stress away with actress Danica McKellar (who I will forever remember as Winnie Cooper on *The Wonder Years*). Danica's mom, Mahaila McKellar, is a certified meditation instructor. She leads viewers through guided imagery and mindfulness mediation segments that calm my body down when I'm stressed. I try to do one of the three short segments each morning. It's a great way to start off my day with peace.

◎ Hip Hop Abs **www.beachbody.com/hiphopabsdotcom**

This Website link will direct you to an infomercial and sales letter, which are a bit "hypey." But look past the marketing. *Hip Hop Abs* has cool music and is a blast to work out to. Exercise is not about punishing our bodies, it's about moving in ways that make us happy. In the words of *Hip Hop Abs* fitness guru Shaun T., "Tilt, tuck, tighten, squeeze; by the time you're done, that's all you'll need."

◎ Tae Bo **www.billyblanks.com**

Okay, okay, all the exercise DVDs I've mentioned so far are a bit "girly." As my husband said, "C'mon, give the guys some love. We're not about to do a downward-facing dog with Rodney Yee and his Speedos." My husband started doing Tae Bo about two years ago and swears by it. It's fun, energizing and challenging. There you have it, guys, no excuse to not sweat off some stress!

◎ The FIRM **www.firmdirect.com**

Regular exercise is a great way to ward off stress, increase energy and boost body confidence from the inside out. My favorite DVD picks are *Power Yoga*, *Cardio Dance Slim Down*, *Aerobic Body Shaping* and *Ultimate Calorie Blaster*.

Movies

◎ *Accepted*

This movie is great: when a high school burnout discovers he's been rejected from every college he's applied to, he creates a fake university in order to fool his overzealous parents. Absolutely hilarious, and a reminder that big things can happen when you pursue your interests and passions.

◎ *Field of Dreams*

One of my favorite movies, and I don't even like baseball! A reminder to us all that sometimes we need to ignore the naysayers of the world and just "build it"—whatever our heart desires, that is, even if it is a baseball diamond in our own backyard. Our hard work will pay off, even if it's in a way that we least expect.

◎ *Finding Forrester*

Another great example of how authentic success is earned through persistence, passion and surrounding yourself with mentors. This film also shows us how mentorship works both ways. Sometimes the student can impact the mentor in a way that's life changing.

◉ *The Devil Wears Prada*

Besides all the fashion talk, which I love, recent college graduate Andy Sachs (Anne Hathaway) has to decide whether her success portfolio is worth a workaholic lifestyle as a co-assistant to a demanding fashion magazine editor. Is the devil the lure of the job, the expensive clothes or Andy's inability to realize that she has free will?

◉ *The Pursuit of Happyness*

A great example of how success is earned through persistence, passion and an unwavering commitment to your dreams and your family. Money does not equal happiness, but the sense of accomplishment you feel after beating the most brutal odds can sure make you want to smile … and cry.

◉ *Rudy*

We can't always get what we want in life, but sometimes the ones who never stop trying end up realizing even greater dreams than the ones they originally trained for. Learning is the point of an education, and Rudy's lessons on and off the football field are sure to make you cry … even the guys (just ask my brother).

Kristen's Picks

Let's start with TV shows:

◎ This is a much older show and for a bit younger audience, but *Even Stevens* featured Ren, the oldest "perfectionist" sibling, who sometimes took herself too seriously. Though her disturbing organization skills usually led to success, her younger brother and his ability to take on the world in an unorthodox style is the star of the show. He may not have the perfect grades, but he can solve any problem, make light of every situation and still have time to make fun of his sister for being such a geek.

◎ In *Gilmore Girls*, Rory struggles to get accepted to an Ivy League school while maintaining a social life. Multiple times each season, it's brought up that Rory needs to relax and take time for herself. And have you met her friend Paris? Paris is funny because Paris needs to chill.

◎ *Home Improvement.* Wilson's character is a wise fellow. Brilliant in all walks of life. He's mysterious. He's funny. He's a lifelong learner!

◎ We've all seen *The Simpsons*. Part of why Lisa is so funny is because her obsession with school can become unrealistic.

As for movies ...

◎ *School of Rock.* (If you can forget the fact that the plot is a rip off of *Sister Act 2*...) All of the students are working toward winning the Battle of the Bands. They don't end up winning, but they learn from the experience. Music has allowed the kids to feel better about themselves. And they've discovered something they love doing that they can do for the rest of their lives: music.

◎ Have you ever seen *Teaching Mrs. Tingle*? It probably rates only one star, but the characters end up holding their teacher hostage all because one student got upset over a less-than-perfect grade.

Appendix E

Contributors

Thank you to Campus Calm U's Student Success and Happiness Experts!!

The dynamic and diverse individuals you've heard from throughout this book are my friends, mentors and business confidants. Campus Calm could not continue to reach students nationwide without their lasting support and guidance. I would not have been able to create a business that I love had I not surrounded myself with these AMAZING role models.

What do we all have in common? A passion to help students succeed! Check out the Campus Calm blog www.campuscalm.com/blog to catch our experts' tips, articles and words of wisdom. Learn how to stress less today and channel that wasted energy to create your happy and successful tomorrows.

Without further ado, meet my experts and friends.

Twentysomething Career Expert

Meet Alexandra

Alexandra Levit is the founder and president of Inspiration@Work, a career consulting firm. A former nationally syndicated career columnist with Tribune Media Services and a current blogger for HuffingtonPost.com and Getthejob.com, Alexandra has authored several books, including the popular *They Don't Teach Corporate in College: A Twenty-Something's Guide to the Business World* (Career Press 2004), *How'd You Score That Gig?* (Random House 2008) and *Success for Hire* (ASTD Press 2008). Her career advice has been featured in more than 800 media outlets including the *New York Times*, the *Wall Street Journal*, *USA Today*, National Public Radio, ABC News, Fox News, the *Greg Behrendt Show*, the Associated Press, *Glamour*, *Cosmopolitan*, and *Fortune*, and her articles regularly appear on the home pages of CNN, MSN, and Yahoo!.

Known as one of the premiere career spokespeople of her generation, Alexandra regularly speaks nationwide at conferences, universities, and corporations including ABN AMRO, Campbell's Soup, CIGNA, the Federal Reserve Bank and Whirlpool—on workplace issues facing young employees. She leverages a youthful appearance and a casual-but-no-nonsense style to influence twentysomethings from the credible perspective of a peer who has recently been in their shoes. Her platform is based on the principle that, in school, twentysomethings simply aren't taught the lessons required for business world survival and success. By introducing audiences to the types of challenges they'll face as young employees, she enhances their productivity and career potential.

Recently, Alexandra has also been called upon to speak to corporate C-suite audiences and Baby Boomer and Generation X managers about intergenerational talent issues. Specifically, she teaches strategies for working effectively with the new crop of twentysomethings—known as the Millennials—that in the next 5-10 years will make up the majority of the workforce.

Alexandra also has 10 years of experience providing integrated marketing communications solutions for Fortune 500 companies. She graduated from Northwestern University and resides in Chicago, Illinois with her husband Stewart and new son Jonah.

Learn more about her at **www.alexandralevit.com**.

Fitness Expert

Meet Amy

Amy Lademann is the founder and president of Beyond Motion, Inc., a wellness and personal development company based in Naples, Florida.

Beyond Motion is dedicated to helping people create balance between body, mind and soul and live their healthiest life possible. Beyond Motion offers personal training, Pilates, yoga, Nia, functional fitness, nutritional counseling and lifestyle coaching through private and group settings as well as weekend retreats. The Beyond Motion group and their partners are recognized experts in their chosen fields and are located throughout the United States, Canada and Mexico, providing exceptional service and uncompromising quality to enhance your life.

Since 2001, Amy has promoted balanced living and the connection between body, mind and soul in various print publications and on TV. In 2002, she was selected by The Nia Technique to teach Nia at an exclusive spa in Europe, and since then she has been involved with opening studios and developing and enhancing mind/body programs in Colorado, California and Florida.

Now residing in southwest Florida, Amy has been featured in the *Bonita Banner*, *Natural Awakenings* magazine, *e' Bella* magazine, and the *Naples Daily News*. Amy introduced Nia to southwest Florida and developed the Pilates program for one of the region's most prestigious wellness facilities.

As owners of Lademann Sports & Fitness, Amy and her husband Rick were honored by *GulfShore Business* magazine in their "Top Forty under Forty" edition in September 2005. In 2007, Amy choreographed and danced in the Gulf Shore Playhouse production of *Romeo and Juliet Revisited*. In August of 2008, Amy was honored as one of southwest Florida's top 10 trainers in *GulfShore Life* magazine. Her speaking engagements include events for private banks, chiropractors, spas, yoga and Pilates studios, fitness facilities and a host of other businesses.

To learn more about Amy and Beyond Motion, please visit **www.Go2BeyondMotion.com**.

Teen Parenting Expert

Meet Barbara

Barbara McRae, MCC, is a nationally known Master Certified Coach and a recognized expert in professional career and life coaching as profiled in *BusinessWeek* magazine, *USA Today*, the *New York Times* and elsewhere. Barbara coaches Millennials to live the life of their dreams. She has been featured in various media outlets, including radio, TV, national magazines and newspapers.

As a former human resources senior executive and corporate trainer, Barbara has twenty-plus years of experience advising, developing and training all levels of professionals and management personnel in both public and private sectors (business, government, health care). She designs and delivers a full range of coaching and training programs, including career satisfaction, communication, leadership and optimal performance. Barbara is also a leadership coach with Coaching.com of The Ken Blanchard Companies, a global training and development company. Major clients include General Electric, Anthem/Wellpoint, Towers Perrin, DREYFUS, Bank One, and the EPA.

Barbara is a bestselling author of *Coach Your Teens to Success*, a former newspaper columnist, and host of *Bridging the Gap* radio show.

Barbara has a BA in International Relations and is a Phi Beta Kappa graduate of Beloit College. She taught at the University of Ohio. Barbara earned her Master Certified Coach credential (highest distinction) from the International Coach Federation—the gold medal standard in professional business coaching.

Barbara lives in Colorado with her family where they enjoy the grandeur of the Rocky Mountains. For more information visit: **www.enhancedlife.com**, **www.smartmirage.com**, and **www.teenfrontier.com**.

Time Management Expert

Meet Beverly

Beverly Coggins, professional organizer, has been organizing herself and others for over 30 years, inspiring her authorship of the *1-2-3...Get Organized* series.

"Organization is my passion, not as an end in itself, but as a means to an end. When my home, office and life are organized, I have more time and energy to devote to my family, my friends and faith," observes Mrs. Coggins.

She lives with her husband in Ohio, where they are foster parents to teenage girls. They have two grown daughters.

To learn more about Bev, visit her website at
www.1-2-3getorganized.com.

Youth Entrepreneurship Expert

Meet Brandon

In the year 2000, at the early age of 10 years old, Brandon L. Griffin started his first business, BLG Publishing (originally Griffin Household Press). At this time, BLG Publishing provided only small desktop publishing solutions (e.g., business cards, brochures, etc.). Brandon started his second business venture, Quality Web Solutions, at the age of twelve. For five successful years, Quality Web Solutions provided web development services, and in 2007 Brandon merged the business into BLG Publishing. BLG Publishing continues to offer the popular web development services under the QWS Online division.

In 2004, Brandon began to speak nationally to youth, motivating them to think of entrepreneurship as a way to successfully use their interests, skills and knowledge. At a national conference for young entrepreneurs, Brandon announced the launch of www.FyeBye.com, a Website for young people who were interested in business. Through FyeBye (For Young Entrepreneurs By Young Entrepreneurs) Brandon's mission was to share with other youth the knowledge he gained when trying to start a business at a young age. In 2006, after two years of planning and preparation, BLG Publishing launched the first issue of *FyeBye Magazine*, the first national business publication with content written by youth.

Brandon is a recent graduate of West Side High School (Gary, Indiana) and is studying business at Purdue University – Calumet (Hammond, Indiana).

Brandon has been featured in *Black Enterprise, NAACP Crisis Magazine*, and *Indiana Business Magazine*. He was awarded Youth Entrepreneur of the Year by each of the following organizations: Indiana Black Expo (IBE), Illinois Institute for Entrepreneurship Education (IIEE), NWI Small Business Development Center (SBDC), Small Business Administration (SBA) and the National Federation of Independent Business (NFIB). Brandon was the first person under the age of 18 to be inducted into the Society of Innovators.

For more information about Brandon or his charitable fund, The Brandon L. Griffin Foundation—A Fund of Tides Foundation, visit **www.ContactBrandon.com**.

Body Image Expert

Meet Courtney

Courtney E. Martin is a journalist, film-maker and teacher. She has written for *Newsweek*, the *New York Times*, and the *Village Voice*—among other publications—and has been featured on *Today*, MSNBC, Fox News and PBS; in *Seventeen*, *Glamour*, *Family Circle* magazines; and on radio programs across the nation. She is currently an adjunct professor of Women's Studies at Hunter College and lives in Brooklyn, New York. Her recently released book, *Perfect Girls, Starving Daughters*, was called a "hard cover punch in the gut" by Arianna Huffington and "a smart and spirited rant that makes for thought-provoking reading" by the *New York Times*. The paperback *Perfect Girls, Starving Daughters: How the Quest for Perfection is Harming Young Women* was released in September 2008.

When she isn't working, which is not nearly enough of the time, Courtney is daydreaming about playing the blues harmonica, cooking dinner with her big brother or making video documentaries with her boyfriend in Lefferts Gardens, Brooklyn. Oh, or conspiring to create unselfconscious dance parties.

Learn more about Courtney and her work at **www.courtneyemartin.com**.

Twentysomething Survival Expert

Meet Christine

 Christine Hassler left her successful job as a Hollywood agent at 25 to pursue a life she could be passionate about. But it did not come easily. After being inspired by her own unexpected challenges and experiences, she realized her journey was indeed her destination. In 2005 she wrote the first guide book written exclusively for young women, entitled *Twenty-Something, Twenty-Everything: A Quarter-life Woman's Guide to Balance and Direction* (New World Library).

Today, Christine supports both men and women in discovering the answers to the questions: Who am I, What do I want, and How do I get it? Christine is a life coach with a counseling emphasis specializing in relationships, career and self-identity. Her expertise is centered on the twentysomething years of life.

Christine began her evolution as a twentysomething expert with a Los Angeles discussion group for twentysomethings struggling with questions about themselves, their careers and their relationships. As she continued her investigation of herself and others, she began to craft a road map detailing how to transform "twenty-something" into "twenty-everything." Christine has dedicated over six years to researching and speaking about this rite of passage.

A professional speaker, Christine leads seminars and workshops for audiences around the country. She has appeared on *Today*, CNN, and

PBS, as well as various local television and radio shows, speaking about life issues and Expectation Hangovers™—a phenomenon she identified and trademarked.

Christine's newest book, *The Twenty-Something Manifesto* (New World Library 2008) stems from her experience counseling twenty-somethings.

Christine's training is from the Communication Arts Company and master's program in psychology at the University of Santa Monica. Christine received her undergraduate degree from Northwestern University where she was initiated as a Kappa Alpha Theta. She serves on the executive board of the Sirens Society, a non-profit organization of proactive women dedicated to making the world a better place through philanthropy and business.

Christine is a yoga enthusiast, travel junkie, wine and food enthusiast (even vegetables!), and loves to be outside. She lives in Los Angeles with her husband, Chris.

Learn more about Christine and her work at
www.christinehassler.com.

College Planning Expert

Meet Dave

As CEO, president and founder of Next Step Publishing, Inc., a company that helps students with college, career and life planning, David Mammano is responsible for daily operations, which includes supervising and mentoring his staff, student volunteers, advertising sales and editorial, as well as and long-term strategic planning.

David expanded the company's core product, *The Next Step Magazine*, from a distribution of 10,000 copies in Rochester, New York in 1995 to more than 1 million readers and Web users in more than 20,000 U.S. high schools and at www.next-STEPmag.com.

In 2006, The Association of Educational Publishers (AEP) gave *Next Step Magazine* two Distinguished Achievement Awards, one in Whole Publication Design (Young Adult) and the other Most Improved Publication (Young Adult).

David also produces a quarterly newsletter, *Brand University* (**www.Brand-University.com**), which helps educational professionals learn more about effective branding, advertising and marketing.

In 2004, David published his first book, *101 Things You Can Do To Become an Outstanding Young Adult*. He also recorded an audio CD for college-bound teens and their parents, *College Planning in 30 Minutes*.

A Rochester, New York native, David graduated from the University at Buffalo in 1991 with a bachelor's in communications/advertising. He is also a graduate of the human relations training program at the Dale Carnegie Institute.

David's board activities include chapter founder of YEO Rochester (Young Entrepreneurs' Organization) and Nazareth College's Entrepreneurial Partnership.

Volunteer activities include Junior Achievement and offering resources to the James P. Wilmot Cancer Center and Golisano Children's Hospital.

At his Upstate New York home, David enjoys the company of his wife, Luisa, and their children, Gianluca and Melania.

David's hobbies include reading, cooking, eating, exercise and repeated attempts at humor.

For more information about David, visit his website at **www.nextSTEPmag.com**.

Mental Health Expert

Meet Hilary

Hilary Silver is a Licensed Clinical Social Worker (LCSW) and Certified Addictions Counselor (CAC) with a private practice in the metro Denver area. She specializes in anxiety, depression, transitions and adjustments, relationship conflict and intimacy, and identity formation. Her philosophy and approach to helping her clients centers on her belief that true happiness and inner peace is achieved when we are living authentic lives; being intentional in our decisions and making choices that honor our true selves. The process of therapy is the journey to understanding, accepting and loving the truth of who we really are as individuals.

Hilary is an eclectic therapist, employing a model called *integral psychology*, which integrates many therapeutic models including cognitive behavioral therapy, psychodynamic, strengths-based, Jungian, internal family systems and many more therapy models. She is also trained in eye movement desensitization reprocessing (EMDR), a neuro-based intervention for mitigating symptoms associated with trauma.

Hilary earned her master's of social work (MSW) from the University of Denver and her bachelor's degree in anthropology from the University of Kansas. She has circled the globe twice on her own, visiting 14 countries in parts of Europe, the Middle East and Southeast Asia and teaching English in Japan for one year. She uses her unique post-college experiences to motivate and inspire her young adult clients to start early in their quest for creating the life they deserve.

For more information about Hilary, visit
www.hilarysilvertherapy.com.

Forever Friend of Campus Calm

Meet Joe

Joe Martin is a nationally known speaker and respected university professor, author and educational consultant.

At the age of 24, he became the youngest faculty member ever hired to teach at a state university in Florida. He also has the distinct honor of being the youngest professor at his institution to ever be nominated twice for the Distinguished Teacher's Award. Joe has taught students at all levels in K-12, including Title I, alternative education and gifted students. He also trains more than 15,000 teachers and administrators each year.

Joe has addressed more than 750 organizations, associations, businesses, colleges and universities and public school districts, helping hundreds of thousands of students and staff members across the country achieve more, live and serve more passionately and maximize their potential. The Association for the Promotion of Campus Activities selected Joe as its national College Speaker of the Year. And Joe was nominated Lecturer of the Year by *Campus Activities Magazine*.

Joe is also the founder and president of RealWorld University (**www.RWuniversity.com**), an award-winning student success Website designed to help students meet the personal and professional challenges of college and life. Joe is also the host of a radio talk show, called *Good Teachers*, that provides educators and parents with strategies to help them motivate, inspire and connect with students. He's also the creator of www.NewTeacherUniversity.com, a Website designed to help retain, train and support new and beginning teachers.

Joe has made several guest appearances on both television and radio, and he's been featured in several newspapers across the country. Joe is also the author of seven books, including *Tricks of the Grade: Street-Smart Strategies for Acing College, Good Teachers Never Quit,* and *Stop Parenting & Start Coaching.* He also serves as a guest columnist for three national publications: *Student Leader Magazine, The Black Collegian,* and *Education World.*

For more information about Professor Joe visit:
www.professormartin.com.

Career Planning Expert

Meet Lauren ...

She's young, she's energetic, she's full of great career advice and she loves coaching college students through their first career search! Students know her as their Résumé Girl, but she delivers far more than just résumés—she's also a coach, speaker, and author.

The Résumé Girl, Lauren Randa Hasson, a Phi Beta Kappa and *magna cum laude* graduate of Duke University, is no stranger to hard work—she completed a triple major in electrical engineering, computer science, and economics in just four years! This dedication to hard work followed her into corporate America where she landed her first job as an investment banking analyst with Morgan Stanley and quickly climbed the ranks to become the lead researcher at one of the world's largest hedge funds. But her true passion resided in working with college students to help them land their first job. So in 2006, she said *sayonara* to her lucrative day job and signed on full-time to be a college career coach.

Since that fateful day, she has coached students from all over the United States, presented frequent seminars to student organizations and even authored a Career Search Organizer. So, whether you are a student looking to land your first job, a student organization officer searching for a seminar speaker or anyone else who wants to help college students navigate the treacherous waters of their first career search, The Résumé Girl would love to hear from you. In fact, she would like you to have her personal email address: **Lauren@TheResumeGirl.com.**

Check out Lauren's website at **www.theresumegirl.com.**

Recent College Graduate Expert

Meet Nancy

Nancy Barry is a speaker, author and Generation Y (Gen Y) expert. One of her passions is helping twentysomethings be successful in their careers. Nancy is the author of *When Reality Hits: What Employers Want Recent College Graduates to Know.* In her book, she shares the secrets to success—mastering "soft skills" in the workplace. She tells twentysomethings what managers want them to know but don't have time to tell them.

Nancy has the opportunity to speak on college campuses across the country and helps her corporate clients get their new recruits off to a great start. She also loves speaking to business leaders about Gen Y—who they are, what they want, what makes them different from other generations and how to manage them. Nancy understands Gen Y—she's raised, hired, mentored and coached them.

Prior to launching her own company in 2005, Nancy served as vice president/community services for *The Dallas Morning News* and WFAA-TV. She is a member of the National Speakers Association, National Association of Colleges and Employers and National Association of Female Executives.

Nancy has been interviewed on numerous national radio shows and has appeared on WFAA-TV, Fox and KTVT-TV. She's been featured in *The Dallas Morning News, Dallas Business Journal, Waco Tri-*

bune Herald and *The Eagle*. Nancy has also written articles for numerous magazines, including *jobpostings, Southern Vanity* and *Richardson Living*.

A native of Dallas, Nancy is the proud mother of two children. Her son, Chris, graduated from Yale University and her daughter, Lauren, is a freshman at Samford University.

For more information about Nancy and *When Reality Hits*, visit her website at **www.nancybarry.com**.

Nutrition Expert

Meet Natalie

Natalie Butler has always been a food enthusiast, and even in childhood was nicknamed the "food police" by her family. She was always aware of what other people were eating and would voice her concerns if she didn't agree with their portion sizes or food choices. Natalie's innate sense of balanced eating combined with family members who were struggling with digestive issues made nutrition a deeply interesting field of study. Natalie graduated with a bachelor of science in food, nutrition and dietetics and recently completed her dietetic internship through Marywood University. She is currently a Registered Dietitian. She is a member of the American Dietetic Association, Austin Dietetic Association, Nutrition Entrepreneurs, Weight Management Dietetic Practice Group and the Sports, Cardiovascular and Wellness Nutritionists (SCAN) Dietetic Practice Group.

After being diagnosed with irritable bowel syndrome (IBS), Natalie began learning about the importance of digestive enzymes for digestive health. She began taking a daily enzyme regimen specific for IBS and began noticing improvements immediately in her digestive function. Within four months, she had recovered from IBS and was able to integrate all foods back into her diet. This personal experience prompted Natalie to study, read and research information about supplemental enzymes in order to help others.

Since then, Natalie has gained experience in the retail food industry and health coaching services through working at Whole Foods

Market and other established wellness companies. Her well-rounded, holistic view of nutrition and health has become the foundation for her own practice, which has allowed her to consult individuals, families, groups and businesses on all aspects of nutrition and health. In addition to working with clients, Natalie writes nutrition articles for several research companies and renowned Websites, is featured on radio programs and is currently working on several nutrition-oriented books and cookbooks. In an effort to reach more people through new media outlets, Natalie has a growing array of nutrition and educational videos posted on YouTube, MetaCafe, Google Video, Yahoo Video, and many other Websites.

Natalie is inspired by helping others achieve their goals and knows that the primary way of doing this is by living what she preaches, so it is her utmost priority to be healthy, active and fit.

For more information about Natalie, visit her website at **www.nutritionbynatalie.com**.

Mental Health Survivor Expert, Campus Calm

Meet Ross

Ross Szabo is the director of youth outreach for the National Mental Health Awareness Campaign (NMHAC). Ross seeks to use his personal experience with mental disorders to raise awareness and provide a positive example for young people nationwide.

After he was diagnosed with bipolar disorder at age 16, Ross was hospitalized in his senior year of high school for wanting to take his own life. Ten months later, he was forced to take a medical leave of absence from American University and was hospitalized again due to a relapse. Ross returned to American University in the fall of 2000 and began to use his broad understanding of mental health to educate others. Ross graduated with a bachelor of arts degree in psychology with honors from American University in May of 2002.

During the past five years, Ross is the only person in the country who has spoken directly to over half a million young people in high schools and colleges about mental health issues. He has influenced the youth of America about the importance of combating the stereotypes that surround mental health. Ross also encourages young people to express themselves and seek help for their problems. His message of individuality and acceptance among youth is making an impact, as he has received tens of thousands of thank you letters from young people.

Ross has made many appearances nationwide and reached millions in media opportunities. He was named the 2007 Best Male Performer of the Year and 2006 Rising Star Speaker of the Year by *Campus Activities Magazine,* which recognized him as one of the best speakers in the country on the college speaking circuit.

Ross has spoken to many national youth organizations, been the keynote speaker at multiple national mental health conferences and he has participated with Tipper Gore and former Surgeon General, David Satcher in "Healing the American Spirit: A Town Hall Meeting of the National Mental Health Awareness Campaign," which focused on the mental health issues surrounding the September 11, 2001 terrorist attack on America.

In addition to numerous Website and newspaper articles, Ross has been featured in *Parade Magazine.* He also wrote a story for the October, 2002, edition of *Seventeen Magazine.* Ross has appeared on CNN, MTV, CNBC and CBS, has been interviewed by National Public Radio and CNN Radio and has been a guest on numerous radio teen talk shows. The Buffalo, New York PBS affiliate WNED turned his high school presentation into a television program called "What's on Your Mind." Ross has recently written a book titled, *Behind Happy Faces; Taking Charge of Your Mental Health: A Guide for Young Adults.*

Ross currently lives in Los Angeles, California. Learn more about him and his work at **www.behindhappyfaces.com**.

Campus Calm Editor

Meet Lori

Lori Mortimer is a writer, editor, instructional designer, and lifelong learner who never had a solid career plan and still doesn't. And yet, she's always had enough work to keep her more than busy. A few years ago, in an effort to strike a better work-life balance, Lori left her office job to work from home as the founding editor of *Student Health 101*™, a digital, interactive wellness newsletter for college students. Currently, Lori freelances part-time while helping her children grow, learn, and play as homeschoolers. She loves the outdoors—mostly in the warm weather. Once the mercury drops below 50 degrees, you'll find Lori bundled up inside somewhere, preferably with a warm child on her lap and a good book in her hand. She lives in Massachusetts with her husband, kids, Chewy the Boston Terrier and a large litter of dust bunnies.

Learn more about her work at **www.lorimortimer.com**.

Thank you to my AWESOME Campus Calm interns!!

In addition to surrounding myself with my team of experts, I am SO LUCKY to have been blessed with the world's greatest interns, Alexa Roman and Kristen Szustakowski. These young women teach me every day about what it means to be a passionate lifelong learner who knows how to have fun! It's true that an intern can teach the mentor as well. So don't ever think you have nothing of value to offer a working professional just because you're a college student or a new graduate.

Alexa contacted me as a recent college graduate looking to diversify her portfolio. She showed me that she was passionate about learning, and equally as important, that she was passionate about helping students. She set up Campus Calm's Facebook page. She showed me how to type an emoticon to stick my tongue out at someone (by the way, it's :-P). She wanted to try her hand at writing. All I can say is, "Wow." Alexa, you are a gifted writer. Add that to your background in film and art, and you can do anything you want in life. I'm in awe of your courage to take risks and try new things.

And Kristen. My talented English major protégé who keeps me on my toes and brings sunshine to the occasional gray day. When I give Kristen a writing assignment, she turns it around in two days and then apologizes for taking so long! When I joke with her that I'm not a slave driver and that I don't expect my deadlines to be met in 24 hours, she responds, "But Maria, it's not work, it's fun. I love, love, love writing, and I love, love, love learning." How can you argue with that?

Kristen, if you want to open a bookstore someday "where there isn't a Barnes & Noble around the corner ... or Fox Books if you've seen *You've Got Mail!*" then I'll be your first customer. And if you want to write an interactive book of quizzes, I'll gladly write your foreword. Or if you want to retire young to a beach and write the great American novel, I'll join you with some sunscreen and my laptop. Thank you for being you. ☺

Without further ado, meet my interns.

Meet Alexa

Alexa Roman has split her time living in the four corners of the United States, but when asked where her hometown is, she will reply "Atlanta, Georgia" with no evidence of a southern drawl. She graduated *magna cum laude* from Emory University with a bachelor of arts in visual arts and art history. Currently on track with her lifelong dream of becoming a filmmaker, Alexa resides in Los Angeles and works in the film and television industry as an art department coordinator. Eventually, Alexa hopes to go back to school for a master's in a design specialty and change the world without using rose colored glasses. She loves everything urban, including *Metropolis* magazine, concrete sidewalks, small apartments and riding the bus with people you don't know.

If you want to tell Alexa about your new favorite band, then you can reach her at **alexa@campuscalm.com**.

———— ⑥ ⑥ ⑥ ————

Meet Kristen

Kristen Szustakowski grew up in Buffalo, New York. She is an English major and communications minor at SUNY Fredonia*. Besides reading and writing, Kristen likes hiking, knitting, silly pens and puppies. After graduating in May 2009, she might get her master's in English, or she might go to law school or she might get a job. She might do something she hasn't even thought of yet! (Yay opportunity!) She would also love to buy a pug and a jeep and move to New Mexico.

Say "Hey" to Kristen at **kristen@campuscalm.com**. If you ask nicely, she may even send you a photo with her newly dyed pink hair. ☺

———— ⑥ ⑥ ⑥ ————

---

* *Since the first printing of* Campus Calm University *in 2008, Kristen graduated from college and has since been promoted to Campus Calm's Creative Direction Assistant.*

Acknowledgements

In addition to my Campus Calm experts and interns, I have many other people to thank (I feel like I'm delivering an OSCAR acceptance speech and the music is starting to play). Well, too bad because these people need some serious thanking!

First, I would like to thank Canisius College, my alma mater, for opening my eyes to a world committed to lifelong learning. Dr. Barbara Porter, you were my angel career counselor (and life coach) through college and when I was a recent college graduate. My mother directed me to you after freshman orientation when you said to her, "I LOVE undecided English majors. You tell Maria to come see me!" I hope you know how much you did to change my life! Eileen Abbatoy, you jumped right in where Barbara left off and have been a wonderful career counselor to me even as an alumnae seven years out of college.

I would also like to thank all my professors and staff in the English and history departments, especially Dr. Tom Reber, Dr. Jane Fisher, Dr. Julie Gibert, Dena Bowman and Dr. Nancy Rosenbloom. Dr. Bruce Dierenfield, thanks for being the *only* professor in four years to give me a "B," even though I wasn't very happy with you at the time. And because I decided to juggle a double major and a minor while working both on and off campus, I'd like to thank Eileen Niland and the counseling staff at Canisius for calming me down when I was ready to snap. Counseling centers at all colleges are underfunded. You reach out to help students as best as you can. We appreciate it!

Okay, moving on to life after college. ☺

Every single person who ever inspired me to keep writing even when life got hard, you know who you are. I will mention a few: Bill Paterson, Dawn Bracely, Jennifer Nelson, Jerry Goldberg, Joe Kirchmyer, Julia Rosien, Kathryn Radeff and Sherry Handel.

A special thanks to Sheri McConnell, my business coach, for showing me step-by-step how it is possible to make a living by creating a business that I love. I'm forever grateful for every person I've learned from through Sheri's organizations, The National Association of Women Writers, Create Your Association and the International Association of Web Entrepreneurs.

My friends

To my amazing friends, I'm sorry I can't name you all, but know that I love and appreciate you. Marty Brown, thank you for reading all my words and providing excellent feedback from the male perspective. Lyndsey D'Arcangelo, you cheer me on through all my writing successes, and I am honored to cheer on your writing successes as well. And Lisa Nasca, my AWESOME friend and marketing consultant. When I was launching Campus Calm, I'd invite Lisa to my apartment, cook her dinner and then pump her for conceptualization advice. Whenever Lisa leaves my apartment, my poor husband has more design work to do!

My family

I'm blessed to have been born into a huge Italian family in Buffalo, New York (a city on the dawn of revitalization that has MUCH more to offer the world besides snowstorms and Super Bowl losses). While some people barely know their cousins, I grew up with a bunch of the greatest first, second and third cousins on the planet. But since I'd need to write a second book to name everyone, I'll just say "Thank you" to my entire extended family of grandparents, godparents, aunts, uncles, cousins and now in-laws for instilling in me the true riches of family.

To my grandfather, the late Richard E. Pascucci, thank you for teaching me that life is so much more meaningful when you do what you love. Thank you for telling me shortly before you left this world, "I'm proud of you. I hope you write another article." Not only did I write another article, *Grandpa*, I wrote a book!

To my brothers, Rick, Joe and John, thank you for instilling me with the uncanny ability to be able to laugh at myself … that and how to throw a mean spiral in a football game. I love you all even though we have that non-verbal "no hug" rule.

To my sister-in-law Beth, thank you for always listening to me, reading my work and letting me know that you think I'm courageous. It helps to hear it every now and then! To my beautiful nieces, Ella, Coura and Lily, I hope that my written words will someday inspire you to be fearless lifelong learners, secure in the knowledge that happiness is the ultimate success.

To my parents, Rick and Barb, thank you for loving me unconditionally and always telling me that I could be anything I wanted to be in this world. Thank you for always being proud of my accomplishments, but also for letting me know that I am more than the measure of those accomplishments. I love you!

And finally, the one who needs the most thanking …

My husband, Shaun Maciejewski. In the thirteen years that you've been my boyfriend, fiancé and now my husband, you've been my rock, my confidant and my greatest cheerleader. Since you've been blessed with unmatched computer, print and Web design skills, you've also had the curse of being my slave. Campus Calm would not exist without the generous help you've offered me after you return home from your day job. This book would not exist without your help (doesn't this book look fantastic?!). Even though we have weathered some hard times (because no relationship is perfect ☺), the good far outweighs the bad. I look forward to growing up with you ... and yes, even growing old with you. I love you!

To my readers (okay, last "finally" I promise)
When I was thinking of creating Campus Calm, I knew there had to be other students and new graduates out there who, like me, believed that there must be more than one prescribed path to success and happiness. Who were tired of hearing that success is just about who you know and how you look on paper. Who wanted to create the type of success paved by joy and purpose.

And you do exist. You, my Campus Calm community, continue to inspire me each day through your letters and amazing feedback. I love you all!

Now in the words of my husband as he was working on Appendix D for the layout and design of this book: "Stop talking already! Save some words for the next book. You're giving away the farm."

Smiles,

Maria

About the Author...

Maria Pascucci, the college student's Stress-Less Life Coach, is the founder and president of Campus Calm and The International Campus Calm University student association. *Campus Calm University* won a gold medal in the 2009 13th Annual Independent Publisher Book Awards. Recognized as a leading authority on college stress, Maria speaks to college audiences on universities across the nation.

As the founder and president of Campus Calm, Maria gives voice to the secret practices, concerns and conversations of a generation of young men and women who believe that it is acceptable, even necessary, to sacrifice health and happiness in pursuit of perfection. A former college perfectionist, summa cum laude graduate and stressaholic, Maria is a trailblazing young entrepreneur on a mission: to spread a dose of "Campus Calm" to stressed-out students world-wide. Campus Calm has been featured in *The Chronicle of Higher Education* and has attracted subscribers from all around the world.

Maria's website is **www.campuscalm.com**.

Fast Facts About Maria

Occupation: Lifelong learner.

Biggest Strength: Too stubborn to get a 9-to-5 job, but disciplined enough to be my own boss.

Biggest Weakness to Embrace: To this day, I still sometimes try too hard, then become really upset when things don't work out the way I want them to. My lifelong battle to embrace imperfection has paved the way for me to launch Campus Calm. It's my calling.

Favorite Color: Fire-engine red.

Favorite Ways to De-stress:
◎ Exercise
◎ Meditate
◎ Paint my toenails ☺
◎ Color in children's coloring books
◎ Walk in the woods
◎ Sleep
◎ Call a good friend
◎ Hug my hubby
◎ And when nothing else works, I cry. I always feel better after a good weeping session, usually while watching a chic flick like *Dirty Dancing* or *Little Women.*

Favorite Thing to Write: The naked truth.

⑥ ⑥ ⑥

Index

Campus Calm Social Networking

Join us at your favorite sites ...

Help spread the word about Campus Calm by joining us on the following social networking sites. Tell your friends about us too!

Visit **www.campuscalm.com/networking**

Campus Calm College Talks

Programs to help students survive college stress and create *authentic* success and happiness

Maria Pascucci is available for:
- Lectures (anytime of year)
- Orientation, welcome week and back-to-school programs
- Student leadership gatherings and honor student programs
- Career day / job fair
- Summer programs
- Club events
- Commencements / graduations
- Any other function where your students would benefit from a youthful, energetic speaker.

> *As a current college student, I know what the meaning of "stressed-out" is. After attending Maria's lecture, she taught me to remove the word "can't" from my vocabulary, and instead think about how something can/should be done. Her organization offers support for students and teaches them to "chill out." I feel more relieved and stress free after attending her presentation, and wish she taught a Stress Management class at my school!*
>
> *Brigid, Sophomore, Canisius College*

Students: contact your campus student activities office to let their staff know you want Campus Calm at your school!

Bring Campus Calm to your school...

Welcome Week & Orientation Package

...featuring 2 campus presentations for both students and parents!

◎ **Stressed-Out Students: A Blueprint to Create Your Campus Calm**

◎ **Parents: 5 Stress-Busting Statements Your College Students Need You to Say Today**

——— ◎ ◎ ◎ ———

◎ **When 'A' Equals Anxiety: Help for Stressed-Out Students**
Perfect for mid-terms, finals and anytime your students need relief from perfectionism.

Visit **www.campuscalm.com/speaking** to learn more about these and other available presentations.

Mention this page to receive 10% off your booking

Campus Calm's Favorite Nonprofits

I started Campus Calm to help high school and college students become stress-resistant, with a goal to eliminate academic perfectionism. I'm sad to say that the problem doesn't begin in high school. Stressed-out children displaying perfectionist tendencies contact me as well. Elementary and middle school students need help. It's time we all Challenge Success.

Championing a Broader Vision of Success for Youth

Challenge Success supports parents and schools who are willing to set the bar high for children, and who understand that real success encompasses:

◎ Character
◎ Health
◎ Independence
◎ Connection
◎ Creativity
◎ Enthusiasm and
◎ Achievement

Please visit **ChallengeSuccess.org** to join their mailing list, learn about upcoming conferences and events, volunteer opportunities and ways to donate to help children reach their full potential.

changing the conversation about mental health

Active Minds, the nation's only nonprofit organization dedicated to utilizing the student voice to raise mental health awareness on college campuses. Since its founding in 2003, Active Minds has become the young adult voice in mental health advocacy and the organizational catalyst for student-based mental health awareness on college and university campuses. Active Minds' chapters are changing the conversation about mental health on college campuses throughout the United States and Canada.

Please visit **www.activeminds.org** to join their mailing list, learn about upcoming events, find information on how to start a chapter on your college campus, find volunteer opportunities and ways to donate to help stop mental health stigma on college campuses.

Like Campus Calm?

Check out our student association at **CampusCalmU.com**

What is Campus Calm U?

Campus Calm U is an international member benefit training program designed to help you gain all the "real world" life and success skills you need but aren't taught in the classroom.

Peek inside the CampusCalmU syllabus:

- Life 101
- Time Management 247
- Nutrition 123
- Twentysomething Survival 209
- Celebrate You 301
- When Reality Hits 365
- And more!

Who is the International Campus Calm U membership for?

High school students, traditional and non-traditional college students and recent college graduates.

Quick Order Form

Order Online: www.campuscalmbook.com

Email Order: orders@campuscalm.com

Postal Order: Fill out the form below and mail it to:

Campus Calm
446 Parker Avenue
Buffalo, NY 14216

Name _____

Address _____

_____

City/State/Zip _____

Phone _____ E-mail _____

Credit Card # _____ ❏ Visa ❏ MasterCard ❏ American Express ❏ Discover

Exp. Date _____ CSC Number* _____

Signature _____

Quantity: _____ x $19.95 each = $_____

Shipping for first book = _____ $3.95

Shipping: _____ x $2.00 for each additional book = $_____

Total = $_____

If paying by check, please make payable to Campus Calm.

* For MasterCard or Visa, the CSC Number is the last three digits in the signature area on the back of your card. For American Express, it is the four digits on the front of the card.

Campus Calm University Press